THE LITTLE BOOK OF LOONY DICTATORS

A COLLECTION OF AUTHENTIC ANECDOTES ABOUT THE WORLD'S MOST PSYCHOTIC DESPOTS

KARL SHAW

ILLUSTRATIONS BY CHRIS ALTHAM

Copyright © Karl Shaw 2011

All rights reserved. No part of this book may be reproduced or transmitted in any form or by any means, electronic or mechanical, including photocopying, recording, or by any information storage and retrieval system, without written permission from the publisher.

Sensible Shoes Publications

By the same author:

The World Encyclopedia of Lies and Utter Fibs

Royal Babylon: The Alarming History of European Royalty

The Mammoth Book of Tasteless Lists

5 People Who Died During Sex

*Curing Hiccups with Small Fires:
A Delightful Miscellany of Great British Eccentrics*

CONTENTS

1. PSYCHOPATHS
2. PARANOIACS
3. KLEPTOCRATS
4. MEGALOMANIACS
5. STAND BY YOUR MAO
6. DICTATOR LIT: THE DESPOTIC MUSE
7. SPORTING DICTATORS
8. LEADERS AT LEISURE
9. DEAD DICTATORS

CHAPTER ONE
PSYCHOPATHS

Indecent proposal

Idi Amin sold doughnuts by the roadside before enlisting as a private in the King's African Rifles of the British colonial army in Uganda. A popular regimental sportsman, he was always the first to jump to attention and salute flag and monarch. To most of the British officers he was 'a splendid chap, though a bit short of grey matter'. A British diplomat in Uganda concurred; Amin was 'virtually bone from the neck up and needs things explained in words of one letter'.

When Amin took control of Uganda in 1971, the occasion passed by with barely a murmur of dissent from the international community, which believed him to be semi-literate, stupid and arrogant – but harmless. It didn't occur to them that Amin was also dangerously insane until, in the interests of better relations with Britain, he volunteered to marry the Queen's daughter Princess Anne.

Execution soundtrack

During Christmas celebrations in 1975, the president of Equatorial Guinea, Macias Nguema, had 150 political opponents rounded up by soldiers dressed in Santa Claus costumes, then shot in the Malabo football stadium, while loudspeakers played Mary Hopkins' *Those Were The Days*.

Taste for sadism

The Dominican Republic's longest serving president Rafael Trujillo was a torturer par excellence, in whose name a variety of methods were employed, including slow-shocking electric chairs, an electrified rod known as 'the cane' (very effective on genitals), nail extractors, whips, tanks of bloodsucking leeches and 'the octopus', a multi-armed electrical appliance strapped to the head. Trujillo's most respected torturer, a dwarf known as Snowball, specialized in biting off men's genitals.

Dissent in the ranks

When Saddam Hussein's war with Iran was going badly and morale was low, he called a meeting of his cabinet ministers and told them he was considering resignation. Most took the hint and insisted that he stay on.
His health minister alone took him up on the offer and agreed that Saddam should step down. Saddam coolly took him into the next room, shot him in the head and sent the man's butchered remains home to his wife in a shopping bag.

Gorilla warfare

In the mid 1920's the Soviet leader Josef Stalin enlisted his top animal-breeding scientist, Ilya Ivanov, to help rebuild Russia's depleted Red Army. Ivanov was instructed to turn his skills from horse and animal work to the quest for a new super-warrior by creating a regiment of hybrid half-men, half-ape. Uncle Joe told him: "I want a new invincible human being, insensitive to pain, resistant and indifferent about the quality of food they eat." Ivanov set off for West Africa with $160,000 to conduct experiments in impregnating chimpanzees.
Ivanov's experiments in Africa were a failure and experiments using monkey sperm in human volunteers back n the USSR

were similarly fruitless. Ivanov persuaded a Cuban heiress to lend some of her monkeys for further experiments, but when the New York Times got hold of the story she quietly withdrew her offer. The disgraced scientist was sentenced to five years' jail, which was later commuted to five years' exile in the Central Asian republic of Kazakhstan in 1931 where he died of a stroke.

Tête à tête

The Haitian dictator 'Papa Doc' Duvalier claimed he could predict the future from his late night conversations with a severed human head, which he kept in a cupboard in the presidential palace. It belonged to one of his former army officers Blucher Philogenes, leader of a doomed CIA-backed invasion of Haiti in 1963.

Keep your friends close and your enemies closer....

The Ethiopian dictator Colonel Mengistu Haile Miriam kept his under the floorboards of his office. This was where police found the remains of his predecessor, the former Emperor Haile Selassie, in 1992.

Making a point

The Dominican dictator Rafael Trujillo always signaled the imminent death of an inner-circle adviser by awarding him the Christopher Columbus medal. It became something of a tradition after the first recipient of the medal died from tetanus when Trujillo inadvertently stuck him with the pin.

Smokin' Joe

Josef Stalin was short and misshapen, born with webbed toes on his left foot. He was also scarred by smallpox; court artists were warned to favour his right profile because it bore fewer pockmarks.

His height also rankled with him and he always wore platform heels to appear taller. Stalin chain-smoked cigarettes, but liked to be seen in photographs pulling pensively on a pipe. The pipe, an important part of his image, was a prop to disguise another deformity; when he was a child he was run over by a horse and cart and as a result of his injuries suffered septicemia, leaving him with a permanently crooked left arm.

Stalin's aides learned to anticipate his moods from gestures he made with his pipe and there were various warning signals of a black temper. If he stroked his moustache with the stem of the pipe, he was in a good mood. If the pipe was unlit, this was a bad sign; If Stalin put the pipe down, an explosion was imminent.

Not to be sneezed at

At an Organization of African Unity summit meeting in 1975, Idi Amin entertained his fellow African presidents by demonstrating how to suffocate someone with a handkerchief.

Punishing schedule

By the time Alfredo Stroessner, the son of a Bavarian brewer, seized power in 1954, Paraguay had seen off thirty-four presidents in fifty years. Stroessner immediately declared a national 'state of siege', then thoughtfully renewed it every three months for the next thirty-four years, making his the longest unbroken rule in South America in the 20th century - second only to North Korea's Kim Il Sung as the world's most durable despot.

Stroessner tortured or killed an estimated 200,000 people during his thirty-five-year rule. He was a leading participant in Operation Condor, a clandestine terrorist campaign against leftists, documenting his torture sessions in a 5-ton archive known as 'the Terror Files'. He was a workaholic, starting his day at 4am by giving orders from his bed to have political opponents hurled from planes, or bound in wire and fed to the piranhas in the Rio Paraguay, regularly working on past midnight.

Stroessner's secret police were known as the puragues – literally, 'the hairy footed ones' - a reminder that their raids were stealthy and brutal. Stroessner's security chief, Pastor Coronel, decorated the walls of his torture chambers with swastikas and pictures of Hitler, Mussolini and Franco. The tasteful torturer also introduced classical music to his 'sessions', to drown out the screams of his victims. Coronel once had the Secretary of the Paraguayan Communist Party torn apart with a chainsaw, to the accompaniment of a polka. The entire proceedings were relayed to Stroessner down the telephone, to ensure that he missed none of the details.

Brotherly love

In 1978 Idi Amin, while covertly planning a full-scale invasion of neighboring Tanzania, tried to lull the country's President Julius Nyerere into a false sense of security with a telegram: "I want to assure you that I love you very much, and if you had been a woman I would have considered marrying you, although your head is full of grey hairs. But as you are a man, that possibility does not arise."

High Hitler

Adolf Hitler was prone to temper tantrums, earning the nickname amongst his subordinates 'carpet biter'. His personal physician Dr. Theodor Morell recorded that the Führer would turn white with his jaws tightly clenched and his eyes dilated; a sign for everyone in his entourage to panic because the fits were usually followed by an order to dismiss or execute someone. Hitler's mood swings were exacerbated by a variety of minor ailments, including stomach cramps and chronic insomnia, which Morell treated with a regimen of seventy-four separate medications. These included mercury and lead compounds known to cause mental deterioration, and Dr. Köster's anti-gas

pills, a mysterious mixture of strychnine and belladonna.
Morell also prescribed 'golden' tablets containing huge amounts of caffeine and the highly addictive amphetamine pervitin, large doses of which are known to cause disorientation, hallucination, convulsion and coma. In September 1940 Hitler threatened to bomb England with a million kilograms of explosives. He later amended the figure to 400,000 kilograms because the original quantity, arrived at under the influence of Morell's pharmacology, on reflection struck him as excessive. According to a 47-page wartime dossier compiled by American Military Intelligence, Hitler took methamphetamines before his final meeting with Italian fascist leader Mussolini in July of 1943, during which he apparently ranted non-stop for two hours.
Morell's successor, Dr. Geising, found that Hitler had been cumulatively poisoned over a period of many years by a variety of drugs in a 'truly horrifying concentration'. Geising was not blameless either: in 1944 he treated Hitler's cold with a 10 per cent cocaine solution and in his last days gave him large quantities of cocaine drops for an eye complaint.

The enemy within

Idi Amin was a cannibal, albeit a reluctant one: he said he found human flesh 'too salty'. The American satirical magazine *The Onion* once ran a story headlined:
'IDI AMIN PRAISES FORMER UGANDAN DEFENSE MINISTER AS 'DELICIOUS'

No Marx for geography

Although his troops occupied half the continent, Josef Stalin had a limited grasp of European geography. He didn't know that the Netherlands and Holland were one and the same and no one in his inner circle dared put him straight.
It was the same with his speeches; if he mispronounced a word or a name his cohorts always repeated the mistake - no one ever

corrected him.

In 1936 the Soviet film chief Shumiatsky was granted permission to record a Stalin speech. When his officials listened to the recording for the first time they were horrified to find that the quality was poor; there were background noises, gaps and jumps.

There was also an anxious discussion about their leader's voice, which sounded distinctly 'tinny'. They concluded that something sinister had happened at the recording plant and that saboteurs had deliberately wrecked Stalin's voice. The NKVD was sent in and the 'guilty' were punished.

Dr. Death

The Malawian dictator Dr. Hastings Banda liked to boast that he fed his political opponents to the crocodiles, but he was not always to be taken literally. In 1983, three of Banda's cabinet ministers and a member of the Malawi parliament died in a mysterious 'car accident'. Only several years later did it emerge that the victims had their heads staved in with tent-peg hammers. He also had a letter bomb sent to the exiled opposition leader Attati Mpakati.

Amin's shopping spree

In January 1971 Idi Amin went to Britain to buy a dozen Harrier jump jets, mysteriously introducing himself to the Foreign Secretary Sir Alec Douglas-Home as 'Field Marshall Amin'. When Douglas-Home asked him what he planned to do with the aircraft, Amin replied, 'bomb Dar es Salaam' (the biggest city in Tanzania).

Amin was disappointed to learn that the Harriers cost $1.5 million each - more than the overseas aid given annually to the Ugandan dictator's near bankrupt economy. He returned home instead with ten pairs of brown shoes and fourteen kilts costing $1100; Amin's long-standing project was the creation of a personal bodyguard of 6-foot 4-inch Scotsmen, all able to play the bagpipes.

Kitchen cabinet

Jean-Bédel Bokassa, president of the Central African Republic, ordered the murder of one of his cabinet ministers, then served him to his colleagues for dinner. It was only when they were all enjoying an after-meal brandy did he reveal the ingredients to his guests.

The 'Buddhist barbecue'

In 1954 America backed the South Vietnamese politician Ngo Dinh Diem as the best man to keep his country from falling under the control of communism, contrary to the advice of France, who pointed out that Diem was 'not only incapable but mad'.

Diem quickly proved himself as a cruel and despotic ruler with a flair for colourful election fixes. In October 1955 the South Vietnamese were asked to choose between Diem and their former Emperor Bo Dai. When the voters arrived at the polling station they were handed two ballot papers, red for Diem and green for Bo Dai; in Vietnamese tradition, red signified good luck, green indicated bad fortune.

Diem's supporters were also at hand to advise voters to put the red papers in the ballot box and to throw the green ones into the wastebasket; the few who did not take their advice were savagely beaten.

In 1963 six Buddhist monks drew attention to Diem's corrupt rule by sitting down in a busy street, then pouring petrol over their heads and setting fire to themselves. In reply, Diem's sister-in-law Madame Nhu, the nation's de facto first lady as Diem was unmarried, offered to give the monks free petrol "If the Buddhists want to have another barbecue".

Secret weapon

In the 1930's Adolf Hitler tried to persuade the Allies that Germany had a death ray. Leading British scientists dismissed the claim as the ramblings of a madman, but Britain's Air Ministry was equivocal. Just to be on the safe side, the Ministry offered a $1500 prize to anyone who could invent a death ray capable of killing a sheep at 100 yards.

Shehu's suicide

The Albanian dictator Enver Hoxha relied very much on the all-round ruthlessness of his faithful second-in-command and war hero Mehmet Shehu, who once reminded colleagues at the annual party congress: "whoever disagrees with our leadership will get a spit into his face, a blow onto his chin and if necessary, a bullet into his head."

Shehu found this to be literally true. On 17 December 1981 he was found dead in his bedroom in Tirana with a bullet wound to his head. The following day, Tirana Radio announced that Albania's long-time premier had committed suicide 'in a moment of nervous crisis' - a crime under Albanian law.

In fact he had been murdered on Hoxha's orders. According to the unofficial version, Hoxha and the 68-year-old Shehu were enjoying a drink of cognac when the chief of the *Sigurimi* and two burly officers burst in. They held Shehu down, but the chief was too terrified to pull the trigger on Albania's second biggest icon, so Hoxha did it himself.

Histories of wartime Albania were summarily pulped to remove all reference to Shehu's military heroics, with his victories retrospectively reassigned to Hoxha.

Ode to a bomb

China's first successful detonation of an atom bomb in 1964 was marked by several days of wild rejoicing - the only nation to announce the creation of a weapon of mass destruction by throwing a party.

Chairman Mao Zedong, who was very fond of writing poetry for 'special events', celebrated the occasion with a poem:

Atom bomb goes off when it is told.
Ah, what boundless joy.

In the late 1960's Mao confessed to his aides that he secretly hoped the US would drop a similar device on a province of China and kill between ten and twenty million Chinese people. This, said Mao, would prove to the rest of the world just how crazy the Americans really were.

Licensed to kill

When Idi Amin seized power in Uganda in 1971, he promised a swift return to democracy, then promptly murdered all of his political opponents, including an Anglican archbishop, the chief of justice, most of the senior army officers plus a couple of senior cabinet ministers who were probably beaten to death by Amin himself.

Amin handed out a mass-murder contract to his private police force, the State Research Bureau, who rounded up candidates and murdered them, then informed the victims' families that for $200 they would lead them to the body. The scheme was a huge financial success, but neighbors complained about the ceaseless din of machine-gun fire at SRB headquarters.

To keep the noise down, Amin encouraged his prisoners to execute themselves by clubbing each other to death with 16-pound sledgehammers.

Idi Amin's favourite place for disposing of his victims was crocodile-infested Lake Victoria, which was also the source of Kampala's hydroelectric power. Whenever the lights went out, that was a sign that the generators on the lake's Owen Falls Dam were once again clogged with the remains of 'Big Daddy's' enemies.

Class warfare

In 1975 Jean-Bédel Bokassa, president of Central African Republic, announced a new regulation requiring every schoolgirl in the country to wear a blue uniform - coincidentally, of a type identical to those made in a factory owned by one of his seventeen wives.

The new law was unpopular because the uniforms were very expensive and few parents could afford to buy them. One day Bokassa's limousine was stoned by a group of about a hundred protesting schoolchildren. The president had them rounded up and taken to a Bangui prison, where they were beaten to death with clubs. Bokassa joined in the massacre and, according to reports, ate some of the victims.

The show must go on

Before he was eventually shot dead by the head of his own intelligence agency, Park Chung Hee, president of South Korea (1963 - 79) survived several assassination attempts, including one on live TV.

On 15 August 1974, the twenty-ninth anniversary of South Korean independence, he was giving a speech at the Seoul National Theatre to an audience of visiting diplomats and press. A gunman emerged from the crowd and ran down the centre aisle, taking potshots at the president, who took cover by diving behind his podium, occasionally peeping out behind his Ray-Ban sunglasses.

The bullets missed their target, but one fatally struck Chung's wife. Another stray felled a girl from a high school choir, who had been hired to sing at the event. After a brief shoot-out the assassin was overpowered. Park rose from his hideout, waved to the audience and, as his dying First Lady was being carried off the stage, continued his monologue. Afterwards, Park and his guests heard a song performed by the choir, minus one soprano.

Cabinet reshuffle

Francisco Macías Nguema won the first post-independence presidency of the tiny African state of Equatorial Guinea, nicknamed "the Dachau of Africa". Nguema had entire families and villages executed and more than a third of his people fled to other countries to escape his brutal reign, including his wife. Nguema averaged about one political killing per week, including ten of his original twelve cabinet members. He clubbed his foreign minister to death and amputated the fingers of his government statistician because 'he couldn't count'.

The Parsley Massacre

The Dominican dictator Rafael Trujillo was a big fan of Adolf Hitler. He aped his idol by equipping his secret police force with a fleet of black Volkswagen Beetles then acquired his own 'chief of Gestapo' in Colonel 'Johnny' Abbes Garcia. A talented psychopath with a predilection for the occult, Garcia claimed the ability to read his victims' auras while burning them with lighted cigarettes.

Trujillo was inspired by Hitler's racial theories and wanted to 'whiten' the Dominican Republic, although he secretly wore pancake make-up to lighten his own skin, inherited from his black grandmother. In 1937, while attending a party held in his honour, Trujillo received word that some of his spies in neighboring Haiti had been killed. In a drunken rage, he ordered his army to kill every Haitian resident in the Republic. In the ensuing massacre, between 12,000 and 25,000 Haitians were slaughtered.

Trujillo's henchmen however had trouble discriminating between the Haitian blacks and the dark-skinned Dominicans, who worked side by side together in the cane fields. Trujillo devised a test to determine if the cane-cutters were Haitian or Dominican. The Haitians spoke French Creole in which, unlike correct Spanish, the 'r' is pronounced as an 'l'. Trujillo had all the workers, at machete-point, pronounce *perejil* - Spanish for parsley. Those who could not correctly roll their 'r' were condemned as Haitians and butchered on the spot.

Demonstrating his flair for the macabre, Trujillo had the bodies of dead Haitians deposited in Massacre River, a body of water between the two nations so-named after previous conflicts between colonial powers Spain and France.

Stalin's bananas

Stalin's bad-tempered paranoia was exacerbated by badly fitting false teeth and sore gums. He was very fond of bananas, one of the few foods he could enjoy without discomfort.

A Politburo member once presented Stalin with a crate of bananas, but to Uncle Joe's fury, they were unripened. Stalin sacked his Trade Minister Mikhail Menshikov and had the ship's captain responsible for importing the bananas arrested.

Blacking up

On 5 August 1972, after one of his regular 'visitations from God', Idi Amin gave Uganda's 50,000 strong Asian population, mostly businessmen, doctors and nurses, ninety days to leave the country.

The evacuation didn't go as smoothly as he had hoped. A few weeks later, Amin made a radio broadcast and warned: "Some Asians in Uganda have been painting themselves black with shoe polish. Asians are our brothers and sisters. If anyone is found painting himself with black polish, disciplinary action will be taken."

Fouling the nest

After eliminating China's class enemies, Chairman Mao turned his attention to the new public enemy number one – sparrows, or more specifically, the Eurasian Tree Sparrow. According to the Great Helmsman, they were helping themselves to millions of tons of grain each year. Mao's scientists had calculated that each sparrow consumed 4.5kg of grain each year and that for every million sparrows killed, there would be food for 60,000 people. Armed with this information, Mao launched his Great Sparrow Campaign.

It was a popular move with most people; sparrows eat cereal crops and the Chinese loved fried sparrow. Over a period of forty-eight hours about 80 million Chinese took to the streets and fields to eliminate the 'pests', banging woks and gongs until the birds dropped dead of exhaustion. Nests were torn down, eggs were broken, chicks killed and sparrows shot down from the sky. Hundreds of millions of sparrows were killed as part of the campaign, as teams of smiling peasants were photographed standing in front of 20-foot high mountains of dead sparrows; the most prolific sparrow-killers were awarded Mao badges, proud emblems of their revolutionary anti-sparrow zeal.

There was however a downside, as the Chinese people soon discovered. Without the sparrows to control worms and other pests, ecological disaster followed swiftly. Agricultural yields were disastrously low with rice production hit the hardest. Things got so bad that the Chinese government started importing sparrows from the Soviet Union in an attempt to correct the imbalance, but the damage was done: the sparrow cull was a significant contributor to the Great Chinese Famine in which an estimated 30 million people died of starvation.

Mao also urged North Korea's leader Kim Il-sung to copy his anti-sparrow campaign. To humor his ally, Kim promised a "three year plan to punish sparrows", but then conveniently forgot about it.

Lost in translation

To mark the anniversary of his 1977 military coup, Idi Amin invited the recently ousted British Prime Minister Edward Heath to fly to Uganda 'with his band' to play before him during the celebrations. Amin said he regretted that Mr. Heath had been demoted to the obscure rank of bandleader, but noted that he understood that Heath was now one of the best bandleaders in Britain (Ted Heath, no relation to the PM, was Britain's most famous bandleader in the 1940's and 50's.) Amin also offered to assist the ex-PM with a supply of goats and chickens. Heath was well used to Amin's philanthropic gestures. He once started a 'Save Britain Fund', promising shiploads of vegetables to relieve economic recession, and offered to organize a whip-round of Uganda's friends, 'if you will let me know the exact position of the mess'.

Trujillo's revenge

The Dominican tyrant Rafael Trujillo knew how to hold a grudge. His henchmen were prepared kidnap and kill his enemies, even those outside the country.

Jesus Galindez was a Spanish professor of literature and political science. In 1956 he wrote a thesis about some of the more revolting crimes committed by the Trujillo then presented it to the faculty history committee at Columbia University in New York. Unfortunately for Galindez, a copy of the manuscript also found its way onto Trujillo's desk. Twelve days later, Galindez vanished without trace.

His disappearance caused an international incident and was extensively covered in the press, but in spite of an extensive search by the FBI and the New York Police Department his body was never found.

An investigation carried out in 1957 disocovered that two of Trujillo's agents had kidnapped the professor from his Manhattan apartment on Fifth Avenue, drugged him, then bundled him aboard a small private plane. He was then flown to the capital of the Dominican Republic, where he was executed in Trujillo's presence. According to reports, Galindez was shackled by his feet, strung upside down, then slowly lowered into a large pot of boiling water.

Papa's bogeymen

The Haitian dictator Francois 'Papa Doc' Duvalier ran a private militia, the *Tonton Macoutes*, who took their name from a mythical bogeyman who hunts down naughty children and kidnaps them in his bag.

The *Macoutes* were above the law and answerable only to Papa Doc. Most were unpaid but there were many perks with the job. A *Macoute* could take his or her food from the market without paying for it, take free rides in buses and taxis and demand that neighbors bring in their harvest or hand over their belongings, land or homes.

A refusal would be interpreted as an act hostile to Duvalier and a reluctant neighbour could be beaten, imprisoned or killed on the spot, the victims' bodies left to lie in the street. Those who spoke out against Duvalier would disappear at night, or were sometimes attacked in broad daylight. *Tontons Macoutes* often stoned and burned people alive, the corpses put on display, often hung in trees for everyone to see. Family members who tried to remove the bodies for proper burial often disappeared themselves, never to be seen again.

Some *Macoutes* attained legendary status, thanks to their creative achievements in brutality. One such celebrated sadist was Rosalie Bosquet, also known as Madame Max, warden of Haiti's 'death dungeon' Fort Dimanche. She delighted in mutilating the genitals of her male prisoners; she once inserted a living rat into a pregnant woman's vagina.

When 'Papa Doc' died in 1971, his son 'Baby Doc' tried to give his father's much-hated militia a makeover, renaming them National Security Volunteers. The rebranding exercise failed and when Baby Doc was forced to flee into exile in 1986, the public backlash against known *Macoutes* was predictably fierce. Many were subjected to 'necklacing' - they were set on fire by having burning petrol-soaked tires placed around the neck. A few of the less fortunate *Macoutes* were ritually eaten by their killers, their flesh having been marinated in a cheap Haitian rum called Clarin.

The hard chairman

Chairman Mao allowed his favourite high-ranking apparatchiks to sit in comfortable armchairs at meetings; displeasure with out-of-favour government officials was signalled by making them sit through long meetings on hard chairs.

The 'Great Helmsman' however was not always quite so cryptic. Unlike Hitler and Stalin, who liked to keep their more serious attempts at thuggery under wraps, Mao liked people to witness his violence and killings.

At a rally in the centre of Peking he had 200 people shot in the head so that their brains splattered onto bystanders.

Occupational hazards

Idi Amin gave his Ugandan cabinet ministers a license to kill if they felt their lives were threatened by 'unruly crowds or distrusted persons'. He forgot to mention that the biggest threat to their health was the chief executive himself.

Amin's campaign of terror against out-of-favour colleagues often ran into logistical problems. A former government employee Francis Kalimazo was at a wedding when he learned of his own 'death' on the radio; Kalimazo realized that he was part of a backlog.

The wife of an Englishman living in Uganda, Bob Astles, was also surprised to receive a telephone call from Amin, who offered his regret for the accidental death of her husband and told her that she could collect the body from the city morgue. Her husband, who knew nothing of the intended assassination, was standing next to her at the time.

Gallows humour

Josef Stalin liked to while away long meetings by doodling on his sketch pad. Some were crude sketches of the enemies he planned to liquidate. In one sketch, his finance minister Nikolai Bryukhanov was depicted naked and hanging by his genitals. A caption underneath read, "To all members of the Politburo, for all his present and future sins, Bryukhanov should be hung by his balls. If they hold up he should be considered not guilty as if in a court of law. If they give way he should be drowned in a river." Bryukhanov was executed in 1938.

Stalin had a favourite joke at cabinet meetings: "there is a man, there is a problem. No man, no problem". It was always guaranteed to raise a chuckle from his underlings, most of whom ended up being executed on their boss's orders.

Whenever he ran into a commissar he hadn't seen for a while, Stalin liked to quip, 'Hello, haven't they shot you yet?'

Saddam's demon seed

Uday, the eldest son of Saddam Hussein, was the second most feared man in Iraq. He was known for his flamboyant dress sense, which ran to large bow ties, suits in colours to match his luxury cars, cowboy hats and beach shirts.

Uday's taste in clothing was rarely remarked upon; an employee had his tongue cut out after noting that Uday's multi-coloured shirts were "a bit effeminate." He once let off steam by making a group of gypsy singers stand in line, drop their trousers and sing while he fired a machine gun over their heads, watching as they wet themselves from fear.

Uday even fell out of favour with his father when, at a party in honour of Egyptian President Hosni Mubarak's wife, he murdered Saddam's personal valet and food taster in front of horrified guests, bludgeoning his victim with a cane before cutting his throat with an electric carving knife.

Saddam was careful to keep both his sons out of the firing line during Iraq's war with Iran from 1980 to 1988, a conflict that cost Iraq 600,000 casualties. The closest either of them ever got to action was a carefully staged tour of the front in 1982.

Saddam asked for volunteers to lead an attack. Uday jumped into a waiting helicopter and took off, rocket launchers firing in all directions, shooting and injuring a number of his own troops.

Dinner date

Dinner guests at Amin's State House were treated to some unscheduled entertainment by their host in August 1972 when, between courses, their president vanished into the kitchen and returned with the frozen head of his former commander-in-chief, Brigadier Hussein.

Amin shouted abuse at the head and threw cutlery at it, then asked his guests to leave.

Heil who?

According to Adolf Hitler, his greatest stroke of good fortune came thirteen years before he was born when his father, Alois Schicklgruber, changed his name to Alois Hitler. *'Heil Schicklgruber'*, he said, would never have caught on.

PROFILE: IDI AMIN

Born: Idi Amin Dada Oumee in 1925 (exact date unknown)

Died: 15 August 2003 (he once confided to a journalist that God had already told him precisely when he would die; when pressed for details, Amin said the information was "top secret")

Also known as: Big Daddy; Dr. Jaffa; the King of Scotland

Occupation: President for Life of Uganda 1971-79 (full title Lord Of All The Beasts Of The Earth And Fishes Of The Sea And Conqueror Of The British Empire In Africa In General And Uganda In Particular)

Hobbies: erecting statues to his greatest idols, Queen Victoria and Adolf Hitler; crushing the genitals of his opponents with his bare hands

Career highlight: carried to his inauguration as President for Life in 1975 by fourteen white Ugandans to symbolize 'the white man's burden'

Career lowlight: in September 1972 *The Sun* newspaper devoted a whole front page to him with just two words, 'HE'S NUTS'

Significant others: four wives, Sarah, Kay, Norah and Medina plus an estimated 43 children

Style: fetish for Scottish regalia especially kilts and bagpipes

Personality cult status:
patented the word 'president' and banned anyone else in Uganda – including heads of companies, unions and other organisations - from using the title

Whimsical cruelty factor:
the first dictator of the color TV era, Amin ordered the decapitation of several political opponents to be transmitted live on television, specifying that the victims must wear white "to make it easy to see the blood".

PROFILE: JEAN-BÉDEL BOKASSA

Born: 22 February 1921

Died: 3 November 1996

Also known as: Papa Bok: the Ogre of Berengo

Occupation: President for Life of the Central African Republic 1966 - 69

Hobbies: eating the opposition

Career highlights: claimed that he was the 13th apostle of the Catholic Church, secretly appointed by the Pope.

Career lowlight: fled the country in 1979 but forgot to dispose of the contents of his fridge, including the whole frozen body of a schoolteacher hanging on a freezer hook.

Significant others: seventeen wives and 53 children

Style: Napoleonic fixation

Personality cult status: promoted himself from 'President for Life' to 'Emperor' in 1977.

Whimsical cruelty factor:
personally supervised judicial beatings and initiated an early version of the "three strikes and you're out" rule; offenders had an ear cut off for the first two offences and a hand for the third. He once made a point at a public press conference by hammering a journalist into submission with the weighted end of his swagger stick. To combat an infestation of beggars in the capital of the Central African Republic, Bangui, Jean-Bédel Bokassa had them loaded on to planes and dropped into the Ubangi River.

CHAPTER TWO
PARANOIACS

Paying guests

Several heads of state who have visited Buckingham Palace were considered less than welcome for return visits.

The list included Malawi's President Hastings Banda, whose henchmen liked torture by electric shock (1985), King Fahd of Saudi Arabia, whose security services preferred flogging (1987) and President Babangida of Nigeria, whose idea of a political debate was to lock up his opponents (1989). None of these however made an impression quite like that made by the visiting 19th century Shah of Persia, whose entourage barbecued a pig in their suite.

To be fair, the visit of the Ceausescus, Nicolae and Elena, came very close. In June 1978 the Romanian President and his wife arrived in London on a full state visit, human rights abuses in Romania considered less important than Ceausescu's status as a potential customer for British aerospace technology.

It was a very high profile event. The presidential couple were met by a gun salute, then treated to a drive down the Mall with the Queen in the royal landau and full board at Buckingham Palace. Her Majesty was baffled by the discovery that her guests had also brought with them their own bed linen and a host of minders, including a personal food-taster. She was also alarmed by Ceausescu's habit of washing his hands every time he shook hands with anyone, a trick he repeated after shaking hands with the Queen herself.

One morning during the three-day state visit, Ceausescu was seen at 6am walking in the palace gardens with his minders. He assumed that his host had bugged his room (as he certainly would have done to theirs) so the garden was the safest place for him to talk. Ceausescu's security officials also reportedly gouged holes in the bedroom walls looking for bugging devices.

Following a telephoned warning from their immediate previous host, the President of France Giscard d'Estaing, in anticipation of the Ceausescus' arrival at Buckingham Palace, small valuable works of art were temporarily removed from their suite. The French president later complained that lamps, vases, ashtrays and bathroom fittings had mysteriously gone missing from the Elysée Palace; he told the BBC, "it was as if burglars had moved in for a whole summer."

The rest of the visit and the aerospace deal went off without a hitch, until it was time to pay up. Romania was so strapped for cash that, when pressed for the money, Ceausescu offered part payment in strawberries, which, when they arrived in the UK, were mostly rotten.

Health warning

Stalin was a hypochondriac and constantly complained of chronic sore throats, psoriasis and various rheumatic aches.

In 1927 he fell victim to a severe bout of depression and called upon the famous Russian neurologist and psychiatrist Vladimir Bekhterev.

The physician diagnosed 'grave paranoia' and advised Stalin's immediate retirement. It was the last advice Bekhterev ever gave; arrangements for the physician's funeral were made soon afterwards.

Titfer tat

The first of a long line of Paraguayan dictators, Dr. Jose Gaspar Rodriguez de Francia ruled his country from 1814 – 1840, turning Paraguay into a paranoid police state, sealed off from the outside world; no-one was allowed in, no-one allowed out. *El Supremo,* as Francia was known, was constantly haunted by the fear of assassination and created a vast network of spies to flush out potential traitors. He passed an eccentric law requiring men to wear hats so that they could tip them to him as he went by, but in practice, chance encounters with the chief executive were unlikely.

Anyone caught out on the street when he was at large had to prostrate themselves or risk being put to the sword by his escort of armed cavalry. Francia had every tree and shrub in the capital Asunción removed in case they concealed assassins. Eventually *El Supremo* became a total recluse, hiding in his palace attended by just four servants, employing his sister to unroll his cigars to check if they had been tampered with, communicating with the exfoliated outside world only through his barber.

He got rid of his political enemies by sending them in their hundreds to his Chamber of Truth, where inmates were chained to dungeon walls and denied medical care or the use of sanitary facilities. He jailed so many that Paraguay's blacksmiths couldn't keep pace with the demand for shackles.

Francia personally supervised firing squads, but didn't like to waste bullets. If a prisoner wasn't killed at the first attempt, he had them run through with bayonets.

Killer joke

Chairman Mao banned all jokes in China in 1944 under a new catch all offence, 'speaking weird words'. Under the new decree, anything from satire to simple wisecracks could have you arrested as a spy.

Calling the shots

Josef Stalin loved to hold all-night drinking binges, at which he encouraged members of his inner circle to get wildly drunk and make fools of themselves, as he watched and listened while quietly sipping a glass of Georgian red.

He enjoyed making his most senior ministers to dance for his amusement, including the sweating Nikita Khrushchev (Stalin's successor as Soviet leader from 1953 – 64) who was forced to drop to his haunches and perform the *gopak* and the Polish chief of security Berman, who was made to waltz with fellow minister Vyacheslav Molotov.

Drinking games were a big favourite with Uncle Joe. Visitors to his dacha might be asked to guess the temperature outside and then have to drink as many glasses of vodka as the number of degrees by which they were wrong. His functionaries were never sure whether their evening out was going to end with a firing squad.

Nine day wonder

In between his regular trips to a Viennese psychiatrist, the rule of the Burmese dictator General Ne Win was defined by bizarre whims, omens and astrological predictions.

Ne Win was obsessed with numerology, especially his 'lucky number' nine. He staged major events on dates containing the number nine - 9 September became a national holiday. He made his pilots circle nine times before landing his plane and he tore down his old palace and built a new one with 9-foot-high ceilings and every measurement rounded to the nearest nine.

In 1987, after consulting his astrologer, Ne Win withdrew Burma's decimal currency from circulation, introducing banknotes in 45 and 90 kyat denominations, both divisible by the mystically desirable number nine, causing economic havoc and widespread financial ruin.

There were ninety-nine Buddhist monks at hand for Ne Win's

last public appearance in 1988, just before he stepped down.

Napoleon of the South Americas

The gluttonous, bandy-legged Paraguayan dictator Francisco Solano Lopez acquired a classic Napoleonic fixation after being told, during a trip to France in 1853, that he bore a passing resemblance to the late, great Corsican.

When he returned home he immediately set about redesigning Paraguay's military uniforms to look identical to those worn by the French, meanwhile ordering for himself an exact replica of Napoleon's crown. He also took to wearing one hand tucked inside his jacket at all times.

In the grip of Napoleonic delusion, Lopez spent most of his eight-year reign waging a hopeless war on three fronts against his neighboring enemies, Argentina, Brazil and Uruguay. Outnumbered by their combined armies by ten to one, *el presidente* made up the numbers by drafting boys and old men. He once tried to rout the Brazilian army by sending out a battalion of twelve-year-olds wearing false beards.

Lopez trained his troops so hard and for so long that many didn't even live long enough to see a battle. Any show of dissent against the Paraguayan president's increasingly desperate military campaigns brought imprisonment, torture and lingering death. Lopez always fled the battlefield at the slightest suspicion of danger and when he ran his generals were always obliged to flee with him; to have shown less fear than the commander-in-chief was considered treasonable.

As the military position grew ever more hopeless, Lopez organized a spying system which encouraged every third man in his army to spy on his comrades and to shoot anyone who showed any sign of cowardice. Many took the opportunity of shooting their officers first to avoid being shot themselves. Widespread paranoia among the ranks led to many of his men marching into battle backwards, more fearful of their own side than the enemy. When Lopez's most senior commander found himself surrounded and facing certain defeat, he opted to blow his own brains out rather than face his president, but missed, shooting only one eye out.

Convinced of a vast conspiracy to overthrow him, the Paraguayan president ordered hundreds of random executions, including those of two of his brothers and two brothers-in-law, plus scores of top government and military officials and several foreign diplomats. His victims were killed by lance thrusts to save on ammunition.

Suspicious of yet another intrigue against him, this time by Paraguay's aristocracy, Lopez solved the problem by putting all of the sons of his country's ruling class into a single regiment, then sent them on a suicidal attack, unarmed and barefoot; all but two died. At one point, realising the hopelessness of his military situation, he organized a mass suicide pact, ordering what was left of the entire population of his nation's capital to follow him into the jungle, but then he changed his mind at the last minute.

In 1870 at the battle of Cerro Cora Brazilian soldiers caught the overweight and over decorated Lopez, ending his career with a bullet. The war with Brazil had reduced Paraguay's population of 525,000 by 60 per cent, of whom only 28,000 survivors were men.

A Zog's life

In 1924 the newly created state of Albania found a new political leader in the person of Ahmed Zogu, a chieftain of the Gheg clan in the Mati valley.

Zogu began his reign as president, until he was shot and wounded in Parliament and a revolution drove him into exile. Six months later Zogu returned and staged a coup. On 1 December 1928 he accepted the 'illustrious crown of the historic Albanian throne' and declared himself King Zog I. It was an excuse to indulge his weakness for spectacular uniforms; for his coronation he ordered an outfit comprising rose-coloured breeches, gold spurs and a gold crown weighing over seven and half pounds.

The occasion was marked by six days of public holidays and planeloads of confetti were dropped over the capital Tirana. Government officials stenciled 'Long live the King' on the walls of public buildings and shopkeepers were threatened with fines unless they displayed Zog's portrait in their window. In some parts a huge letter 'Z' was burnt on to the hillside.

In spite of these displays of public enthusiasm, King Zog was anything but popular. His struggle to become political master of Albania had been achieved on the back of murder, torture, blackmail and bribery on a scale never before seen in the history of his country.

By 1928 he was involved in as many as 600 *giakmarrje* (blood feuds) with various people he had upset during his leadership. It made him the subject of an estimated fifty-five assassination attempts. Except on national holidays Zog hardly ever dared appear in public. As he was well over 6 feet tall with red hair, he made a conspicuous target in a country where most men were dark and under 5 foot 6.

On very rare occasions when he ventured outside, his mother acted as chaperone - according to the strict rules of the Albanian blood feud, no man can be harmed if accompanied in public by a woman.

Zog spent most of his reign as a recluse in his capital city, Tirana, playing poker and chain-smoking up to 150 cigarettes a day. His nerves were so frayed that on his wedding day he banned photographers' flashbulbs; not once during the ten days' commanded public celebrations did he or his bride dare to appear at the palace window to acknowledge their cheering subjects.

Zog presided over a huge royal family, including six sisters, a half-brother, several nieces and nephews, a queen mother who patrolled the royal kitchen to protect him from food poisoning and an elderly 'godfather', known as 'the scabby one', who carried revolvers in the pockets of his morning suit.

Zog rarely left his country for fear of revolt in his absence, but in February 1931, aged thirty-four, he collapsed with severe chest pains and was obliged to consult a specialist in Vienna. The visit, the first time Zog had left Albania since 1924, was conducted in such secrecy that even some of his most senior ministers were kept in the dark.

The trip resulted in the most famous of his many assassination attempts. On 21 February, as Zog was leaving the Vienna Opera House two gunmen opened fire as he was climbing into the car. The bullets meant for him were stopped by his ADC Topallaj and his minister Libohava. The trial of his two Albanian assailants, Noloc Gjeloshi and Aziz Cemi, was held at Ried in Austria.

Although a police investigation found evidence that the would-be assassins were in the pay of the Yugoslavian government, the men claimed they had acted alone, on impulse. Gjeloshi explained, "When an Albanian has not got himself in hand, he has a revolver in it."

The common touch

The Romanian dictator Nicolae Ceausescu and his wife Elena shared a phobia of germs. The presidential couple went on numerous publicity walkabouts, photo opportunities that required them to shake a few hands and kiss small children, but they were terrified that they would catch a terminal disease from contact with the Romanian masses.

The problem was solved to their satisfaction by their secret police, the *Securitate*, who rounded up a few volunteers weeks in advance and had them locked up and disinfected in readiness for the big day.

* * *

Saddam Hussein also had a paranoid fear of germs. The Butcher of Baghdad was terrified of even the tiniest cut and he gave his doctors precise instructions to determine the perfect germ-free temperature for his office. Saddam's visitors were briefed with a set of rules, including how to shake his hand and the precise distance they should stand away from him; apparently, Saddam preferred to be greeted with a kiss near his armpit.

Among those who shook Saddam's hand, Luna Dawood, whose father was employed by the state oil company, said that the Iraqi leader's cologne was so overpowering that she couldn't to remove the smell from her hand for days and the living-room sofa where he sat smelled so strongly that it had to be given away.

* * *

Benito Mussolini was obsessed with germs; he adopted the Roman-style straight-arm greeting as the fascist salute because he hated shaking hands with people.

Bunker mentality

The Albanian dictator Enver Hoxha lived in perpetual fear of joint invasion by 'Anglo-American Imperialists' and 'Russo-Bulgar revisionists'. In 1950 he ordered the construction of a prototype concrete bunker, complete with a sniper's gun slit with 360° visibility. When the small, mushroom-shaped edifice was complete, Hoxha asked the chief engineer if he was confident that it could withstand a full assault from a tank. He replied in the affirmative. Hoxha then ordered the engineer to stand inside his creation then watched while it was bombarded by a tank.

Fifteen minutes later the shell-shocked engineer emerged, shaken and deafened, but unscathed. Hoxha was impressed and immediately ordered mass construction of the bunkers.

From 1950 until his death in 1985 Hoxha built around 800,000 bunkers - one for every four Albanians - covering the entire countryside and costing from one-third to one-half of his nation's pitifully small resources. It was all to no avail, because no one bothered to invade.

Death sentence

On a visit to China in 1965, the British Second World War hero Viscount Montgomery asked Chairman Mao, "If you died today, who would take over?" Mao replied: "Liu Shaoqi" - then head of state.

When he returned home 'Monty' related this anecdote to the British press, who revealed that Liu Shaoqi was the Number Two man in China. Unwittingly, Monty had signed Liu's death warrant. The newspaper headlines convinced the paranoid Mao that Liu was scheming to take over. Mao promptly had his former comrade arrested. Liu, or as he was now known in China, 'Number One capitalist roader', died in prison, deprived of food and medical attention.

The body politic

Chairman Mao disliked most things Western. He especially hated toilets with a seat and flushing mechanism and refused to use them whenever he was abroad. When Mao went to Moscow in 1949 for Stalin's 70th birthday celebrations - his first ever trip out of China - he insisted on squatting over a bedpan because all the toilets in the Kremlin were of the flushing variety.

Mao's bowel movements were a daily topic of conversation in the highest echelons of the Chinese government. He was so severely constipated that one of his bodyguards had to administer an enema every three days; a 'normal' movement was a cause for celebration among his top officials.

* * *

Security around the North Korean dictator Kim Il-Sung was tight on trips abroad; his aides carried a special toilet with built-in monitoring equipment to keep tabs on his health. It also served another private function, which was to keep the Great Leader's deposits away from the clutches of foreign intelligence agencies; both the American and Soviet secret services were known to place 'traps' in the plumbing of buildings frequented by world leaders.

* * *

According to an actual report written for the US government by Freudian psychologists at the height of World War II, Adolf Hitler's urge to enslave the western world was the result of vigorous potty training.

* * *

The North Korean government website once stated that their leader Kim Jong-il never needed to urinate or defecate. The statement was later removed.

Death and taxis

The Haitian government radio station, Radio Commerce, occasionally interrupted scheduled programs to broadcast the popular song *Di fe den kaill la* - Fire in the house. It was a secret coded signal that they were in the throes of yet another attempt to overthrow their president, 'Papa Doc' Duvalier.

He survived nine attempts to depose him. The first came in 1958 when a gang of eight rebels, including three ex-deputy sheriffs from Miami, Florida and New York, 'invaded' Haiti and advanced on the presidential palace at Port-au-Prince in a stolen jeep.

On their way to the capital however the jeep broke down. Posing as tourists, the invading army flagged down and hijacked a taxi-bus. As no-one was expecting a revolution by taxi, they were able to drive into the Dessalines barracks unopposed and disarm the handful of sleeping soldiers before the Haitian military were even aware of their presence.

The weapons cache they had hoped to find stored at the barracks however had been moved to the palace basement. Papa Doc, who had no idea that only eight men were involved in the invasion, packed his bags and made ready to flee to a foreign embassy. The rebels showed their hand by sending one of their hostages out to buy them a packet of cigarettes; he was captured and the true scale of the invading army was revealed to the embarrassed authorities. Duvalier ordered his troops to storm the barracks and all eight men were executed on the spot.

In 1967 Papa Doc thwarted a coup involving Haitian army officers, led by his son-in-law Colonel Max Dominique. Afterwards, officers of the Haitian General Staff were called to Papa Doc's palace then driven to Fort Dimanche, where they found nineteen of their colleagues tied to stakes. The officers were issued with rifles and under the gaze of Papa Doc, invited to shoot them. The public got to hear about it several days later when the president gave one of his strangest speeches yet: |"Duvalier is going to do something. He is going to take a roll call. Major Harry Tassy, where are you? Come to your benefactor . . . absent. Lieutenant Joseph Laroche . . . absent"... and so on, through the nineteen names.

Then, after a pause, Papa Doc delivered his punchline; "All of them have been shot!"

Send in the clones

The Albanian dictator Enver Hoxha allegedly had a village dentist abducted by his secret police and surgically enhanced to make him appear to be the president's identical twin.

Hoxha's plan was to keep his look alike close at hand in case of an invasion; the double would be sacrificed to enemy soldiers while the president escaped to the mountains.

The double spent ten years in relative luxury in a small compound within the presidential palace and was brought out to stand in for his president at official events every now and then. When Hoxha died and the communists were overthrown, the double was attacked by a mob that thought he was the former dictator's ghost.

* * *

Hitler was rumoured to have employed as many as six doubles including his regular driver Julius Schreck, who often acted as the Führer's double because of their close natural physical resemblance. According to some reports, Schreck died in a traffic accident in 1936; according to another version he died from an abscessed tooth. *Time* magazine once named a second double, Heinrich Bergner, who was killed in July 1944 by a bomb intended for Hitler.

Another Hitler body double who didn't get off lightly was Gustav Weler, who took a bullet to the head around the same time Hitler did, just to keep up appearances. When the Nazi high command learned that the Soviets were approaching, they attempted to confuse the Allies by persuading them that Hitler was already dead. The corpse of Weler, or at least someone who looked very much like Hitler, was found by Red Army troops in Reich Chancellery garden, where they temporarily stopped their march to take pictures and pose with the body. However, according to a servant who was present at the bunker, the dead man was actually just a cook who happened to be sporting a Hitler moustache and was "assassinated due to his strong likeness to Hitler." Weler's (or the cook's) body was taken to Moscow for investigations and buried in the yard at Lefortovo prison.

* * *

Josef Stalin used several doubles, including a man identified only as Rashid who closely resembled the dictator even down to his deep facial pockmarks.

After Stalin's death in 1953 Rashid shaved off his moustache and gradually went bald, but even then the resemblance was so striking that people stopped and stared at him on the street. Some people believed that Stalin had faked his death and gone into hiding among them.

Another look alike, an actor called Alexei Dikiy was hired to live in the dictator's dacha outside of Moscow in the late 1950's when Stalin was seriously ill to fool visitors into thinking that their leader was still in control of his faculties.

A third Stalin double, Felix Dadaev worked as Stalin's body double at public functions, even meeting party officials, and once stood in for Stalin before a parade in Red Square.

Dadaev kept quiet about his work for more than half a century fearing, not unreasonably, that the KGB would come after him if he told anyone about his old job.

* * *

The North Korean dictator Kim Jong-Il routinely hired doubles to carry out some of his more mundane duties, such as regular visits to farms and tractor factories. According to South Korean intelligence sources, the two stand-ins were the same height as Kim and had plastic surgery to enhance the resemblance to their chubby leader right down to his bouffant hairstyle and pot belly.
Some US analysts were convinced that when former president Bill Clinton travelled to North Korea in August 2009 to meet Kim Jong-Il, he actually met a Mr. Kim look-alike.

* * *

Kim Jong-Il developed a fear of triplets after being tipped-off that a triplet was destined to overthrow his regime. He ordered the seizure of all of his country's triplets and placed them in state-run orphanages.

Top dog

Because of his anti-Soviet stance, the Romanian dictator Nicolae Ceausescu was courted by the West and regularly showered with gifts by visiting dignitaries. These presents ran from cars to pets. The British gave Ceausescu a black Labrador puppy called Gladstone, which the tyrant renamed Corbu.
Despite his friendly relationship with the west, Ceausescu was terrified that his ambassadors would defect and only ever |employed people in the post who were not fluent in foreign languages.
The most important job entrusted to the non-English speaking Romanian ambassador in London was a weekly trip to the supermarket to purchase dog biscuits for Corbu, before sending them on to Romania in the diplomatic bag. 'Comrade Corbu' became the subject of much urban myth; Ceausescu

was said to be so fond of his dog that he gave it a house with a telephone and promoted it to the rank of Colonel in the Romanian army.

Bad hair days

The Albanian dictator Enver Hoxha banned beards and long hair, even on visiting foreigners. Albanian-border barbers were employed to snip excess hair from all foreigners entering the country; the degree of hairiness was then noted in police files.

* * *

Park Chung-Hee, the president of South Korea, cracked down on lefty students by declaring an Anti-Long Hair Campaign. His police were authorized to seize hirsute Koreans in the street and shave them right there on the spot.

Park was even tougher on communists; Article 10 of his country's constitution offered prize money to anyone who killed one or caused a communist to commit suicide.

* * *

In 1966 Doctor Hastings Banda became the first president of the newly established republic of Malawi.

An Anglophile with a taste for three piece Savile Row suits and Homburg hats, Dr. Banda worked hard to keep modernity at bay by employing airport barbers to clip long-haired males on arrival; short-skirted female visitors were required at gunpoint to open their suitcases and change into something that covered their knees. Banda spent almost all of his country's education budget on a public school known as 'Eton in the jungle', offering cricket, cold showers and classical education in Latin and Greek. He imposed the local Chichewa as the new official national language - an odd decision even by Banda's eccentric standards, given that he did not actually speak a word of Chichewa himself. Throughout his entire thirty-year presidency he had to communicate with his people through an interpreter.

The bitterest pill

To ensure that his country's population kept pace with that of its two great neighbors, India and China, the Burmese dictator General Ne Win outlawed all forms of contraception. It was a tough assignment for Burmese mothers, outnumbered by their neighbours by forty-seven to one.

* * *

Nicolae Ceausescu took drastic measures to try to double Romania's population in a generation. Every month Romanian women were forced to undergo body searches in the presence of government agents known as the 'menstrual police' to ensure that they weren't secretly using contraceptive devices. Expectant mothers who failed to produce a baby on the due date were arrested for questioning. Women who did not bear children, including those who were incapable, were obliged to pay up to 10 per cent of their monthly salaries. Sex education was also banned; books about human reproduction were classified as 'state secrets' to be read only by doctors.

Ceausescu imposed a 'celibacy tax' on women of childbearing age who failed to give birth to at least four children; no-one dared to point out that Ceausescu's wife Elena had only three.

Consumer-unfriendly

The Albanian dictator Enver Hoxha banned Western pop music, Greek Christian names for babies, kissing on television and foreign travel, to name but a few of his pet hates. Even more puzzling were his bans on private ownership of consumer items including television sets and private cars - luxuries that his country couldn't provide, that no Albanian could ever afford anyway and that few had even seen. No one was allowed to drive a car without a permit and only two permits were ever issued outside of the Albanian Communist Party. In 1992, when Albania was opened to foreigners, there were only 150 cars in the entire country.

However there were very few complaints about the lack of

consumer goods: the penalty for being overheard complaining that the shops were empty was fifteen years' hard labour. Anyone who wasa caught trying to leave the country - mostly by swimming the three-mile channel to Corfu - was shot and their bodies strung up on public display.

Brie speech

Nicolae Ceausescu's father Andrutsa was a notorious drunk. One evening Ceausescu senior was with some friends in a bar in the centre of Bucharest when his son appeared on television making a speech. He told his fellow drinkers not to take any notice of anything his son said because 'he tells nothing but lies'. The following day the bar had vanished and had been replaced by a cheese shop.

North Korean mole

The North Korean leader Kim Il-sung had many accomplishments. He once turned sand into rice and could cross rivers on a leaflet and was said to be descended from Tangun, a divine 'bear-man' who founded their country more than 5,000 years ago.

Kim was always shown in pictures viewed from his left side - propaganda management to hide a large unsightly growth on the right side of his neck. US intelligence experts analysed the Dear Leader's mole and pronounced that it was a cancerous tumor. Predicting his imminent death, they forecast that North Korea would soon collapse or at least suffer mass riots. Against all odds, Kim survived to become the subject of another rumour, this time that he had been run over by a truck and was suffering brain damage.

In 1986 US intelligence experts confidently announced the "assassination of Kim Il-sung", a story that occupied headlines for several days. The episode was quietly forgotten when Kim showed up to meet the Mongolian president a couple of weeks later.

Castro in the crosshairs

The Cuban president Fidel Castro, according to the people who had the job of keeping him alive, survived more than six hundred attempts to assassinate him. The bids to kill Castro began after the 1959 revolution that brought him to power when a CIA agent sent from Paris failed to snuff him out with a cunningly disguised pen-syringe. There were several attempts to kill Castro using explosives. Once, a barrage of shells aimed at the Cuban leader missed him by forty minutes but melted all of the traffic lights in downtown Havana.

On another, three would-be assassins were apprehended while carrying a bazooka across a university campus in broad daylight. When Castro was on a visit to Panama the CIA tried to smuggle 200lb of high explosives under the podium where he was due to speak. Castro's personal security team intervened and the plot was aborted. Some of the attempts to kill him were more fanciful. The CIA recruited one of Castro's former lovers to track him down and finish him off; she was given poisoned pills, which she hid in a jar of cold cream, but the pills dissolved. She toyed with the idea of slipping cold cream into Castro's mouth while he was snoozing, but lost her nerve. On another occasion a poisoned chocolate milkshake was accidentally placed in a freezer; by the time it was offered to Castro, it was frozen solid and had lost its potency.

There were other attempts to prepare bacterial poisons to be placed in Castro's handkerchief or in his tea and coffee, but none got off the drawing board. In 1960 the CIA tried to dose a cigar with a lethal toxin and slip it into his private stash during a trip to the United Nations. They aborted similar plans to load his cigars with explosives, or with an hallucinogenic drug to give him a wild acid trip to embarrass him during a public appearance.

In the most creative plot of all, the CIA hoped to undermine Castro's popularity by planting thallium salts - a powerful hair remover - in his shoes during a trip overseas so that his famous beard would fall out. When the CIA discovered that Castro enjoyed scuba diving, they bought a diving suit and contaminated the regulator with fungus spores, hoping to give him a rare skin disease. The diplomat assigned to hand over the 'dirty' suit accidentally gave him a clean one instead. The CIA also explored the possibility of placing an exploding conch at Castro's favourite diving spot. The plan was to find a shell big enough to contain a lethal quantity of explosives and paint it in bright colours to attract Castro's attention when he was underwater.

Arguably the most visionary scheme to kill the Cuban leader came from General Edward Lansdale, who contemplated invoking Jesus Christ himself in the covert war against Castro. The general hoped to spark a counter-revolution by spreading the word to Cuban Catholics that Castro was the anti-Christ. At the imminent Second Coming, Christ was going to surface off the shores of Cuba on board a US submarine. Devout Cubans, Lansdale explained, would rise up and overthrow their evil leader.

In his autobiography *Shadow Warrior*, retired CIA operative Felix Rodriguez confessed to making three trips to Cuba to assassinate Castro. In 1987 the Iran-Contra committee wanted to know if Rodriguez took part in the CIA's infamous attempt to poison Castro's cigars. "No sir, I did not", he replied, "but I did volunteer to kill that son of a bitch in 1961 with a telescopic rifle."

Unofficially, the CIA abandoned their attempts to kill Castro in the 1980's, but the Cuban leader wasn't taking any chances. He moved address twenty times and gave up smoking in 1985. His apparent indestructibility was much joked about in Cuba. One told of him being presented with a Galapagos turtle. Castro declined the gift after learning that it was likely to live only 100 years. "That's the problem with pets," he grumbled, "you get attached to them and then they die on you".

PROFILE: NICOLAE CEAUSESCU

Born: 26 January 1918

Died: 25 December 1989

Also known as: Comrade Supreme Commander; Genius of the Carpathians; The Conductor

Occupation: President of Romania 1965- 1989

Hobbies: expert on Orwellian repression. Suppressed free speech and travel by introducing the world's first typewriter license, by banning maps and by making it illegal to talk to foreigners. After receiving an anonymous death threat through the post, he ordered his secret police to secure handwriting samples from the entire Romanian population; bear hunting with his Holland & Holland custom British rifle

Career highlights: awarded an honorary knighthood, the Grand Cross of the Most Honorable Order of the Bath by the Queen during his visit to Britain in 1978. Ceausescu responded by awarding Her Majesty the Star of the Socialist Republic of Romania First Class.

Career lowlight: sixteen years later, only hours before Ceausescu's execution on live TV, the British asked for their medal back

Significant others: wife Elena, 'world-renowned chemist and scientist'. Wife Elena, 'world-renowned chemist and scientist' . Twenty-seven close relatives, all holding top party and state positions, including son Nicu, a talented rapist who once escaped prosecution after running his car over a girl whilst drink-driving.

A Romanian intelligence service chief who defected to the West told in his memoirs of a banquet at which he saw Nicu pour Scotch over the foreign minister's head, urinate over a platter of oysters then rape a waitress.

Style: A fussy dresser; convinced that foreign agents were trying to poison his clothes he had the state police make everything he wore for him, including his favorite German-style hunting outfits, under surveillance in a specially constructed warehouse; each garment was worn once then burned

Personality cult status:
a real-life communist version of Mel Brooks' Springtime for Hitler, including large-scale, theatrical public spectacles designed to show the Romanian people that they were living in a socialist paradise where thousands of factory workers gave their bodies to spell Ceausescu's name. Uniquely among twentieth-century tyrants, the Ceausescus had their own 'house style'. Newspapers had to mention the name of their leader no fewer than forty times on every page and always in their own special typeface. The names of Nicolae and his wife Elena had to be written on the same line; no other names could be quoted in the same paragraph, nor were they ever photographed against any background other than red, the approved colour of the Communist revolution

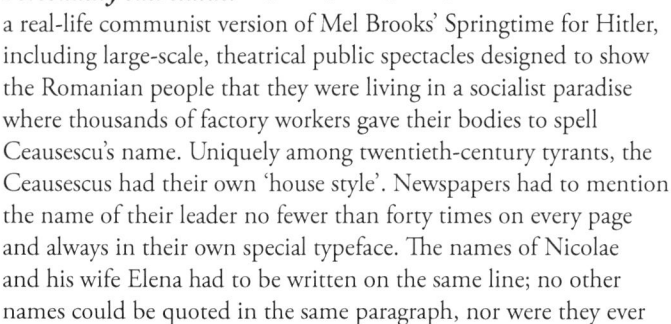

Whimsical cruelty factor:
emptied hundreds of villages or 'renovation', his euphemism for ethnic cleansing. Destroyed a dam and let it flood a nearby village full of Hungarians.

PROFILE: FRANCOIS DUVALIER

Born: 14 April 1907

Died: 21 April 1971

Also known as: 'Papa Doc'

Occupation: President of Haiti 1957 - 1971 (full title, Lord And Master Of This Land of Haiti)

Hobbies: voodoo - took advice on matters of state by sitting in his bathtub wearing a black top hat while consulting the entrails of a dead goat

Career highlights: keeping domestic dissent low and foreign bank accounts high.

Career lowlight: before he came to power spent two years in hiding from the government of the day, dressed as a woman

Significant others: wife Simone, 'Mama Doc'; son Jean-Claude, 'Baby Doc'

Style: black suits and bulging holsters; kept visiting Western journalists on their toes by fingering his desk 'paperweight' (a .45 revolver) and a .357 Magnum he kept under his cushion

Personality cult status: instigated a graffiti campaign claiming 'Duvalier is God'. Six Haitian students responded by painting 'Caca Doc' (Doc is shit) on a Port-au-Prince wall. Dozens of students and their relatives, including several university professors, were arrested and beaten; the six culprits were personally interrogated by the president in his basement room then executed. Papa Doc banned every youth organization in Haiti, including the Boy Scouts

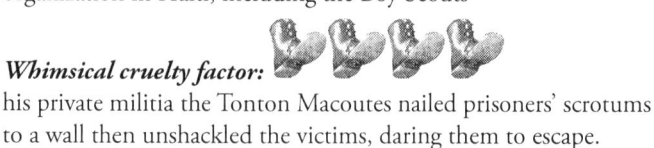

Whimsical cruelty factor:
his private militia the Tonton Macoutes nailed prisoners' scrotums to a wall then unshackled the victims, daring them to escape.

PROFILE: MUAMMAR GADDAFI*

Born: 1942 (precise date unknown)

Died: 20 October 2011

Also known as: Brother General; King of Kings; the Mad Dog (courtesy of Ronald Reagan, 40th US President)

Occupation: President of Libya 1969 - 2011 (full title Colonel Muammar Abu Minyal al Gaddafi, Leader of the Revolution)

Hobbies: marathon speeches, milking cows: in an effort to present himself as a Libyan everyman he kept a model farm with a herd of Friesians

Career highlight: in September 2009 he asked the UN to abolish Switzerland. Tensions had been strained between Gaddafi and the Swiss ever since his son Hannibal was arrested in Geneva for allegedly assaulting two servants

Career lowlights: (1) his interview with John Simpson of the BBC. When the cameraman played back the interview tape, the microphone clipped to the leader's chest had picked up the sound of repeated farting (2) after his overthrow he was dragged out of the drainpipe in which he was hiding and then shot in the face.

Significant others: (1) The Gaddafi Girls - his unique, personal bodyguard of young Libyan females who sport figure-hugging combat gear and inch-long fingernails painted in a deep red gloss. (2) his voluptuous blond long-time Ukrainian 'nurse' Galyna Kolotnytska

Style: revolutionary haute couture including purple and gold designer robes that he changes up to five times a day and T-shirts screen-printed with photographs of African leaders. At a function in Tripoli Gaddafi had to walk up some steps to a podium and appeared to be limping, inviting excited speculation by western journalists that he had suffered a stroke. It turned out that he was breaking in his new Cuban heeled shoes

Personality cult status:
liked to remind everyone that he was a 'man of the people' by pitching up in a Bedouin tent, but his image was everywhere in the streets and in the official media sporting a bewildering variety of costumes including military, Arab and Western with rock-star shades, accompanied by the slogans "If it weren't for you the impossible would not happen," "It is an honour to live in your country" and "Spring for ever"

Whimsical cruelty factor:
confessions routinely extracted by torture methods of all types known since the Middle Ages, according to Amnesty International.

* There are at least thirty-two different ways to spell his surname in English including Kazzafi, Gadafy, Gadhafi, Gheddafi, Qadhdhaafi. The name derives from an Arabic verb meaning to fling, hurl, toss, push, shove, pelt, eject, oust, defame, slander, strafe or vomit.

CHAPTER THREE
KLEPTOCRATS

Mobutu's millions

Before he was overthrown in 1997, President Joseph Mobutu's 32-year rule over Zaire had made him the seventh richest man in the world, when his country was among the poorest. He was so wealthy that he could, had he chosen to, have written a personal cheque to pay off his country's entire foreign debt.
Mobutu's conspicuous consumption was unparalleled. He chartered a French Concorde to fly his family to Europe on monthly shopping trips. He had his pink champagne flown in from Paris, mussels flown in from Belgium and prostitutes delivered from Scandinavia. So he could build himself a model farm in the Zaire jungle, in one year he sent a government jet to Venezuela thirty-two times to bring back 5,000 long-haired sheep.

Exile in Kensington High Street

In 1939, invasion by Benito Mussolini forced Albania's heavily braided despot King Zog and his wife to flee into exile, accompanied by their huge family and a couple of thousand officials.
The Zogs and their huge retinue decamped to the Ritz Hotel in London, where the hall porter was taken aback by the sheer weight of their cases. He enquired whether they contained

anything valuable. Zog replied; "Yes, gold."

Zog found himself in the news when he lost his wallet to a pickpocket in Harrods. By an amazing stroke of good fortune, the wallet was recovered containing £1,000 in cash. The story attracted widespread attention in the press and seemed to confirm suspicions that Zog had escaped from Albania with the entire national treasury.

Later, Zog tried to buy The Times, but when he discovered it was not for sale he settled for the less influential Kensington and Chelsea Post instead.

Zog thought it wise to sell his bright red Mercedes, a wedding present from Adolf Hitler and inconveniently identical to the one used by the Führer himself. Unfortunately, the cheque for £800, which they received in exchange for the car, bounced and the police were called in. The car was located in Scotland, but had been sold on a couple of times and Zog had to buy it back. Zog spent a large part of his exile in California when Ronald Reagan was governor. In 1967 Zog I's only son, Crown Prince Leka, gifted Reagan an elephant he had bought from Harrods.

Going by the book

In the 1980's a Western Christian group sent 20,000 free Bibles to Romania, where president Nicolae Ceausescu had promised to distribute them.

When the Bibles arrived he confiscated the lot and had them pulped to ease a national toilet-paper shortage. The quality of Romanian pulping was so poor that the words God and Jeremiah were still clearly visible on the rolls of recycled toilet paper.

Blood money

The Haitian dictator 'Papa Doc' Duvalier raised corruption to an art form, diverting millions of dollars in foreign-aid money into his own bank account while his country slid into financial ruin - the poorest nation in the western hemisphere.

Although Duvalier pocketed around $15 million a year in foreign aid from the US alone, he was not the most grateful of recipients. He once kept the American ambassador Benson Timmons waiting for five weeks for an audience then gave him a lecture on good manncrs.

Papa Doc's rule of terror and widespread theft, however, was also punctuated by unpredictable, random acts of benevolence. In 1973 a group of trade unionists imprisoned for two years for daring to strike for higher pay, were unexpectedly released and invited to Papa Doc's palace. To their astonishment, each was pardoned and handed an envelope containing a wad of notes.

One of Papa Doc Duvalier's favourite fundraising schemes involved handing out of medals to foreign leaders in exchange for small 'loans'. The Cuban strongman Fulgencio Batista was awarded Haiti's highest (and newly invented) medal in exchange for $4 million.

He also hit upon a way of literally bleeding his own people dry. His militia, the *Tontons Macoutes*, had a daily round up of thousands of Haitians and marched them to the nearest blood bank, where each was given $1 - about a week's wages - in exchange for a litre of blood. The blood was then sent on to the United States, where it was sold for transfusion at $12 a litre.

Royal appointment

When Idi Amin came to power in Uganda in 1971, Britain sent out a Foreign Office minister, Lord Boyd, to congratulate him. Amin requested a signed portrait of the Queen and a royal visit as soon as possible; he assured Boyd that he had already written Her Majesty 'a very nice letter'.

In July 1972 Amin got his wish and went to Buckingham Palace to have lunch with the Queen and her husband, the Duke of Edinburgh, whom he addressed throughout as 'Mr. Philip'.

Upset that he was never asked back, Amin wrote to the Queen

again three years later: "I would like you to arrange for me to visit Scotland, Ireland and Wales to meet the heads of revolutionary movements fighting against your imperialist opprsion."

Unpalatable appetites

While his countrymen endured devastating famine, North Korea's Kim Jong-Il lived the life of a jet-set billionaire.

Perks of the Dear Leader's job included use of a stable of 100 imported limousines, as well as imported professional wrestlers from the United States at a cost of $15 million to entertain him, and chefs flown in from Italy to prepare his pizza.

Thousands of bottles of Hennessy Paradis were shipped to North Korea for the personal consumption of Kim every year, confirming the Dear Leader as the world's biggest buyer of the French cognac, with an estimated annual account of $600,000 to $900,000 since 1992. Kim's annual spend on cognac ($600 a bottle in Seoul) was 770 times the income of the average North Korean citizen.

Costa del psycho

When The Haitian dictator 'Papa Doc' Duvalier discovered that tourism in his country was down by 70 per cent, he was torn between his need for revenue and his natural mistrust of foreign troublemakers.

He hit upon a compromise. After launching a publicity drive to tempt the visitors back, he had the corpse of a dissident flown into the capital Port-au-Prince, where it was left to rot in public. It was strategically placed by an exit from the airport, next to a sign which read 'Welcome to Haiti'.

Power dressing

The Dominican tyrant Rafael Trujillo liked to be known as *El Benefactor*, although strictly speaking, the only beneficiaries of his lengthy rule were actually himself and his immediate family.

In 1955 Trujillo celebrated the twenty-fifth year of his regime with a full year of trade fairs, exhibits, dances and performances culminating in a grand promenade designed to showcase the dictator's daughter, sixteen year-old Angelita, who was crowned Carnival Queen.

One-third of the nation's annual budget was invested in the gala, a large chunk of which was spent on Italian designer Fontana gowns for Angelita and her entourage of 150 princesses.

Angelita's costume was an exact copy of that worn by Queen Elizabeth I at her coronation, complete with brooch and sceptre. The white silk gown had a 75-foot train and was decorated with 150 feet of snow-white Russian ermine, requiring the skins of 600 animals, as well as real pearls, rubies and diamonds. To protect her robe an army of street sweepers scrubbed by hand the central boardwalk of the capital city of Ciudad Trujillo where Angelita's float would pass and her entry was made on a mile of red carpet. The cost of her costume alone was $155,000 (1955 prices).

Permanent President

As well as wide scale theft, 'Papa Doc' Duvalier specialised in colourful election fixes. In 1961 his countrymen went to the polls and found pre-printed at the top of each ballot sheet the words 'Doctor François Duvalier, President'. The votes were counted and it was announced that Papa Doc had been unanimously re-elected on the basis that his name appeared on every ballot paper.

A few years later Haitian voters were asked, 'Do you want your President elected for life?' the answer was a convenient and resounding 'yes'; unsurprisngly, as there was apparently no room on the ballot sheet for a 'no' box.

The Ceausescu Diet

Nicolae Ceausescu tried to pay off Romania's huge foreign debts by exporting almost all of his country's agricultural production, resulting in food rationing and near famine. When he heard reports that his people didn't have enough to eat, he dismissed them as nonsense, remarking that Romanians ate too much anyway.

Eventually he was persuaded that the crisis was genuine so he found a 'solution' to the food crisis however in the revolutionary Ceausescu Diet, a 'scientific' regimen mysteriously free of the protein-rich staples Romanians missed most, especially meat and dairy products.

To demonstrate that production targets were actually being met, Ceausescu staged visits to the countryside where he was filmed inspecting impressive displays of meat and fruit; the film crews alone knew that the food was mostly made from wood and polystyrene.

Pilfering Philippine

As well as appropriating up to a third of all loans to the Philippines in the form of kickbacks and commissions, the light-fingered dictator Ferdinand Marcos also oversaw foreign investment in his country, for a small fee. A *New York Times* report found that a US nuclear power company had paid him tens of millions of dollars in bribes to allow them to build on Philippine land. As it turned out, it was money not well spent: the power station was never used, having been built on top of an earthquake zone.

While Marcos was amassing one of the world's largest private fortunes, inflation in his country rose to 6,000 per cent. To pay his army, which was on the point of rebelling, he issued a 5 million dollar banknote. It was actually worth much less and suspicious shopkeepers refused to take them. In the ensuing riot about 300 people were killed

Let them eat Gogigyeopbbang

In 2000 the North Korean press reported on a remarkable new food 'invented' by Kim Jong-Il called *Gogigyeopbbang*.

Described as "double bread with meat", it was created on Kim's orders to alleviate food shortages. Some observers noted it that was uncannily similar to a hamburger.

Six years later, Kim initiated another culinary revolution when he ordered the breeding of giant rabbits.

Capital gains

Papa Doc Duvalier dreamed of building a new Haitian city, a permanent memorial to his megalomania, called Duvalierville. Naturally, his countrymen were expected to foot the bill. Local businessmen were invited to contribute: those who declined had their premises burned down and looted. Other reluctant donors were imprisoned, tortured and killed.

Another successful fundraiser was the use of roadblocks to collect impromptu tolls. Telephone subscribers were surprised to find that they too had been charged an extra levy to fund the building project, especially as Haiti's telephones had not worked for twenty years.

Unlike the fundraising projects, Duvalierville was not a success and was never finished; most of the money went directly into Papa Doc's bank account.

Eat thy neighbour

While his country was officially rated one of the mostly poverty-stricken in the world, Jean-Bédel Bokassa, ruler of the former French colony Central African Republic, spent a third of his country's annual budget on single ceremony to celebrate his promotion from president to emperor in 1977.

The event required the purchase of 100 limousines and 130 thoroughbred horses and featured four full-sized concrete replicas of the Arc de Triomphe. The guests drank 65,000 bottles of champagne served by an army of waiters imported from Paris and were entertained by a 120-piece orchestra. The Paris-based jeweler Claude Bertrand was commissioned to make Bokassa's crown, which was heavily encrusted with diamonds including a massive 58-carat showpiece. Bokassa sat on a 2-ton solid gold throne made in the form of an eagle sitting upright with wings outstretched, wearing two leopard-skin mantles.

Although all of the world's top political leaders were asked to attend the ceremony, most, including Britain and the US, returned their invitations.

However, several minor foreign dignitaries, including the Prime Minister of Mauritius did pitch up at the capital, Bangui, to sample an imperial banquet featuring 'roast beef'. It was rumoured that Bokassa had arranged to have twelve selected inmates from the local prison butchered and served to his dinner guests.

Baby on board

In January 1971 the dying Haitian dictator 'Papa Doc' Duvalier introduced to the world his successor, his 19-year-old son Jean-Claude, described by a French journalist as "a prematurely overweight sports-car enthusiast" and so slow-witted he was known to his schoolmates as 'basket head'. More optimistically, Papa Doc likened his son to Caesar Augustus, "who was also nineteen when he took on his hands Rome's destinies". Unfortunately, since the dictator spoke mostly in French to his Haitian people, it was lost on about 90 per cent of them who couldn't understand a word he said; the rest assumed it was all a joke.

Three months later the ailing Papa Doc died and 'Baby Doc' Duvalier became the world's youngest dictator. True to family tradition, in his first test at the polls Baby Doc was re-elected with an impressive 99.9 per cent of the vote. Keen to reassure his people that was a genuine democrat, within weeks of gaining power he had posters put up all over Haiti, which read: "I should like to stand before the tribunal of history as the person who irreversibly founded democracy in Haiti." Each was signed: 'Jean-Claude Duvalier, president-for-life.'

In 1981 the IMF gave $22 million to the treasury of Haiti, only to discover two days later that $20 million of this had been withdrawn by 'Baby Doc' Duvalier. Most of the money went on his wife Michele, who spent $50,000 a month to fly flowers from Miami to Haiti and liked to crank up the air conditioning so she could wear her fur coats indoors.

In 1985 discontent with the new regime erupted in food riots Amid rumours that he had fled the country, Baby Doc appeared on television to reassure Haitians that their president was still "strong, firm as a monkey's tail".

The following year, amid further rioting, the Duvaliers threw a champagne party at the presidential palace in Port-au-Prince, bade farewell to friends, then fled into exile on board an American military aircraft, pausing on the way to dig up 'Papa Doc's' remains and remove a hundred million dollars in cash from the Haitian central bank.

During a subsequent investigation of Baby Doc's finances, the authorities raided his Riviera villa, where they caught Michele Duvalier trying to flush a notebook down the lavatory. It contained details of her recent spending: $168,780 for clothes at Givenchy; $270,200 for jewellery at Boucheron; $9,752 for two children's horse saddles at Hermes; $68,500 for a clock; and $13,000 for a week in a Paris hotel.

PROFILE: ADOLF HITLER

Born: 20 April 1889 at Braunau-am-Inn, Austria

Died: 30 April 1935 in Berlin, Germany

Also known as: *der Führer*; Wolf; Carpet Biter

Occupation: Chancellor of Germany 1933-45

Hobbies: watercolor painting and foreign travel

Career highlights: (1) after writing the best seller *Mein Kampf*, a successful European book tour. (2) Voted *Time* magazine's 'Man Of The Year' in 1938

Career lowlight: two rejections from the Viennese Academy of Fine Arts. He blamed it on the Jewish members of the review board, not lack of talent

Significant others: wife Eva Braun; pet dog Blondi

Style: brown shirts and toothbrush moustaches:

Personality cult status:
every child member of the Hitler Youth movement could expect to say 'Heil Hitler' at least 50 and anything up to 150 times a day.

Whimsical cruelty factor:
tendency to order executions when depressed: preferred dogs to people, but still tested a fatal dose of prussic acid on his much-loved Blondi.

PROFILE: ENVER HOXHA

Born: 16 October 1908

Died: 11 April 1985

Also known as: Great Teacher; the Ugly One,

Occupation: President of the People's Socialist Republic of Albania 1945 - 85 (full title Comrade Chairman Prime Minister, Foreign Minister, Minister of War, Commander in Chief of the People's Army (later he added 'Supreme' in front of 'Comrade' and mysteriously started to call himself 'Sole Force')

Hobbies: a committed atheist, had priests buried alive

Career highlight: on a visit to China Hoxha began his speech: "Albania and China are very important countries. Together we make up 25% of the worlds population"

Career lowlight: as a communist guerrilla fighter, forced to subsist on boiled gravel for three years.

Style: more Stalinist than Stalin. Hoxha styled himself on Uncle Joe but then broke off relations with the Soviet Union in 1961 because it was 'too soft'. By that time about 25 percent of Albanian men were saddled with Stalin as a first name.

Personality cult status: when the Enver Hoxha Museum opened for business the Albanian media proclaimed it "a landmark rivaling the Sphinx among the glories of human civilization." Schoolchildren were deployed to spell out slogans on the hillsides in white painted stones such as 'Long Live Enver', 'Enver Party' and 'Albania: Rock of Granite'. Those who fell out of favour were punished with longer messages, including 'Up with Revolutionary Spirit', 'The Worst Enemy Is a Forgotten One' and 'American Imperialism Is Only a Paper Tiger.'

Whimsical cruelty factor:
dismissed his prime minister by shooting him dead over dinner.

CHAPTER FOUR
MEGALOMANIACS

Word to the wise

Idi Amin liked to dispense advice on protocol to his fellow world leaders, from President Richard Nixon to Mao Zedong. He once reminded the Israeli Prime Minister Golda Meir to pack her knickers and told Queen Elizabeth to come to Uganda 'if you want to meet a real man'.

In 1978 wrote to Lord Snowdon after his split with the Queen's sister Princess Margaret, 'Your experience will be a lesson to all of us men to be careful not to marry ladies in high positions.'

Divine intervention

In 1870 Paraguay's President Francisco Lopez declared himself a Saint of the Christian Church. When the matter was put to the bishops of Paraguay, the twenty-three who did not agree were shot. 'Saint' Francisco was duly anointed and the date officially entered into the Christian calendar.

Any witch way

Yahya Jammeh seized power in the tiny west African state of Gambia as a 29-year-old lieutenant in 1994, through the simple expedient of being the first officer to reach the presidential gates during the overthrow of his predecessor.

Since then, Jammeh has displayed a passion for witchcraft over statecraft. After one of his aunts died, apparently the victim of a curse, more than 1,000 "sorcerers" were rounded up at gunpoint by the presidential guard unit, the Green Berets, and forced to drink hallucinogenic poisons designed to 'exorcise' them.

Jammeh is also known for his virulent opposition to gay rights. He once threatened to behead gay people and offered to hunt down and kill anyone who cited the persecution of homosexuals as a reason for seeking asylum abroad.

He also holds some unorthodox medical views. In 2007 President Jammeh disclosed that he was able to cure HIV, AIDs and asthma via a combination of charms, charisma and magic. The president promised that the 'cure' took about three days, after which "I can tell you that he/she will be negative".

Jammeh did not disclose what the treatment involved exactly, other than that patients are not allowed to eat seafood or peppers, but advised that "they should be kept at a place that has adequate toilet facilities because they can be going to toilet every five minutes."

Official Gambian news sources reported that the president's astonishing curative resources had left medical staff "mesmerized and stunned"; Gambian bloggers however reported his medical intervention leaving patients vomiting and in agony.

Red herring

The brutal and erratic Maximiliano Hernández Martínez, President of El Salvador (1931 - 1944) was known as *El Brujo* - the witch doctor- because of his habit of making decisions in consultation with occult powers.

Martínez held regular séances in the presidential palace, during which it was revealed to him that there are five extra human senses - namely: hunger, thirst, procreation, urination and bowel movements. Martinez believed that the colour red has magical healing qualities: he once tried to cure a smallpox epidemic by covering all of the streetlights with red cellophane. He had a higher regard for animals than people: he once noted: "it is a greater crime to kill an ant than a man, for when a man dies he becomes reincarnated, while an ant dies forever."

Martinez fled El Salvador after a popular revolt in 1944 and lived in Honduras for many years, until one of his servants hacked him to death with a machete.

Idi's boots

Idi Amin was fickle in international relations. He was once allied to Israel, a country that awarded him the wings of a parachute commando, which 'Big Daddy' wore with pride on his military uniform. Amin however soon shifted his allegiance to Libya and Palestine, claiming that Israelis had deliberately poisoned the waters of the Nile and were planning to invade Uganda and declare it a Zionist state.

In 1972 Amin phoned Jordan's King Hussein and his cabinet and military commanders in the middle of the night to tell them he had a plan to conquer Israel. His enemies were puzzled when, a year later, he was shown still sporting his coveted Israeli paratrooper wings in his likeness on Uganda's new banknotes.

Amin once refused to attend the Commonwealth Games unless the Queen sent him a new pair of size-thirteen boots.

If the cap fits

The Dominican Dictator Rafael Trujillo was an obsessive collector, especially of neckties; by the time of his death he owned more than 10,000.

As a child however he liked to collect bottle caps and acquired the nickname *chapita*, slang for bottle cap. He hated the nickname and as president he solved the problem by banishing the word from the language.

The last words he heard his killers say just before they

assassinated him were; "this is the end, Bottle cap".

The people's palace

The Romanian dictator Nicolae Ceausescu enjoyed a taste in architecture that made Stalin's look understated.

Ceausescu bulldozed the centre of Bucharest, a city once known as the Paris of the East, sweeping aside historic boulevards to straighten the streets so that the sights of his machine-guns could get a clear line of fire at the approaches to his new residence, The People's Palace, a 1,000 room eyesore incorporating the work of around 700 interior designers.

During construction of the palace - second in size only to the Pentagon and featuring a marble-lined nuclear bunker - the designers ran out of gold for the door handles and used so much marble that they had to invent a synthetic substitute. The palace required the destruction of schools, hospitals, churches and dozens of historic buildings, forcing about 40,000 people to give up their homes in exchange for small apartments in grim, concrete tower blocks. Thin interior walls and bugging devices were standard, drainage was not.

The relocated masses were required to sign paperwork to request the demolition of their houses. Compensation for the lucky ones was a fraction of their actual worth; the less fortunate had to pay for the cost of demolition.

In 1978 Ceausescu planned a welcome speech to new students of Bucharest's polytechnic. His chosen venue was the local park, but he was annoyed to find that where open parkland had once lain, a huge hole had been excavated to make way for Bucharest's new underground station. He simply ordered the hole to be 'removed' until after his speech. Throughout the night, hundreds of labourers toiled to fill in the hole, covering it with grass and trees uprooted from other parts of the city. No-one remembered however to keep the civil engineer in charge of the Bucharest Metro project in the loop; when he turned up for work the following morning he was astonished to find trees and park benches where his station should have been.

Badges for the billions

During his leadership, more than 90 per cent of the Chinese people wore Chairman Mao badges, each embossed with the Great Helmsman's image; estimates of the total number produced range between 2.5 billion and 5 billion.

Most carried the left profile of Mao's head; some showed full frontal views of his head or his body from the waist up and on rare occasions, his whole body.

In deference to the prevailing political mood, badges featuring Mao's right profile were taboo. Each badge had a safety pin with which it could be affixed to clothing, or for the more zealous, directly through the skin.

Cock of the walk

When Colonel Joseph Mobutu took control of the Belgian Congo in 1965 he launched an 'authenticity campaign' to break with his country's colonial past. Everything with a European name was purged and renamed with a new, Africanised version: buildings, people, even the country itself, which became known as Zaire.

Mobutu also banned Western-style clothing and in a unique political fashion statement declared a Mao-style suit, the *abacost*, the new national dress. Western forms of address such as Mr. and Mrs. were forbidden; everyone was to be known as 'citizen'. Mobutu's propagandists had his portrait hung in every shop, bank and business. He also outlawed all wearing of leopard-print hats, except of course his own.

The evening news showed a spectral image of Mobutu arriving to Earth on a magic carpet of pillowy clouds, usually accompanied by stories about his alleged supernatural feats, including the lion he killed with his bare hands at the age of seven and the battle he fought against Zaire's enemies where bullets and spears bounced off his chest. Mobutu always carried a wooden walking stick featuring a carved eagle, a symbol of power that allegedly took the strength of eight normal men to carry.

He was particularly keen that his countrymen knew about his sexual prowess, as shown by the new official title he took for himself, *Sese Seko Kuku Ngbendu Wa Za Banga* – 'the cock that leaves no hen unruffled'.

Seriously fascist

Benito Mussolini was inclined to take himself seriously and was always shown in official portraits looking stony-faced and wearing a military uniform. He vetted every press photo taken of him; on the back of each he scribbled either 'yes' or 'no' followed by a large 'M'. Those that showed him looking jovial or relaxed, rather than stern and straight-faced, were marked 'no'.

Pictures of Mussolini with nuns or clergy were forbidden because he thought this would bring him bad luck. Any photograph that showed the potato-sized cyst on the back of his neck was similarly banned; photographers who accidentally took a picture in which the cyst was visible would have their film confiscated.

In 1937 the English journalist Vernon Bartlett interviewed Mussolini and afterwards sent his draft copy to his office to be vetted. As Bartlett recalled, *Il Duce* made only one only alteration to the manuscript; Bartlett had written, "The Duce's laughter encouraged me to ask another indiscreet question." The word 'laughter' was crossed out. Il Duce, Bartlett was informed, never laughs.

Mussolini's grip on the Italian press also left little room for humour. He especially hated comic strips, which fascists considered alien to the Italian cultural tradition and a propaganda vehicle for Anglo-Saxon democracies. The only American cartoon hero not to be banned was Mickey Mouse, a big favourite in Mussolini's household.

Flying visits

On 24 April 1966 the Ethiopian Emperor Haile Selassie became one of the few foreign heads of state to consent to visit 'Papa Doc' Duvalier's Haiti. Seizing on a rare opportunity to present himself as a world-class statesman, Papa Doc planned a massive and elaborate civic reception. He even 'borrowed' Haiti's few luxury cars and filled in all of the potholes on Port-au-Prince's main thoroughfare, renaming it Avenue Haile Selassie. Papa Doc was disappointed when his VIP declined an invitation to stop over even for one night.

* * *

Although few of his countrymen were allowed to use it, the President of Belarus Saparmurat Niyazov (1985-2006) built an airport, Turkmenbashi International - bigger than JFK but with only three flights a day.

In May 2000 the airport received its most distinguished visitor ever, the Russian President Vladimir Putin. It was only supposed to be a flying visit, but Nyazov was determined to bask in Putin's reflected glory for as long as possible. Putin was said to be furious when, at the banquet in his honour, Niyazov deliberately dragged out proceedings, including forty-two toasts, well past midnight so he could boast that the Russian leader's visit had lasted two days.

La bella lingua

Benito Mussolini launched an anti-swearing campaign with a series of posters all over the country ordering *Non bestemmiare per l'onore d'Italia* - Do not swear for the honour of Italy. Allied spies monitoring Mussolini's radio addresses during World War II were puzzled by the fact that *Il Duce* always referred to the American president, Franklyn Delaware Roosevelt, as Delano. At first they assumed that it was a mispronunciation of FDR's middle name. The mystery was cleared up by an Italian interpreter who explained that *Del ano* translates roughly as Italian for 'asshole'.

Red mist

During the Cuban missile crisis, Fidel Castro was outraged when the Soviet Union backed down from making a pre-emptive strike against the United States.

He wrote a letter to the Soviet leader Nikita Khrushchev calling him a "son of a bitch, bastard, asshole, no balls homosexual".

War record, fabrication of (possibly)

According to his propagandists, over a period of fifteen years the North Korean leader Kim Il-sung fought in more than 100,000 battles against the Japanese in the 1930's, an unlikely average of over twenty battles a day.

The biggest ever box office hit in North Korea is *Sea of Blood*, a wartime musical depicting Kim Il-sung, with some artistic license, as an heroic guerrilla leader with most of the credit for the victories over Japan. It also has a hit song, *My Heart Will Remain Faithful*.

Tall stories

Nicolae Ceausescu was very short, not that it was ever apparent from the photographic evidence of his time in office.

Pictures of the tyrant meeting foreign dignitaries were always taken at a foreshortened angle so that he looked as tall or even taller than his guests. No such measures were necessary for domestic photo opportunities because appointments to his government were made on the basis of height. Ceausescu insisted that his ministers had to look up to him; consequently two of his most senior ministers, Postelnicu and Bobu, were near dwarfs.

The stock photos of Ceausescu in the 1980's also showed him

looking twenty years younger and wrinkle-free, the result of a great deal of retouching, with occasionally bizarre results.

In 1989 he was photographed meeting the Bulgarian dictator Zhivkrov, who was wearing a hat. As Ceausescu was hatless in the original photo the retouchers were required to quickly paint in a hand holding a hat. Unfortunately they forgot to remove one of his real hands; Ceausescu appeared in the newspapers the following morning with three arms.

The two Joes

Stalin liked to compare himself to the great Czars of Russia and joked that he might eventually marry a princess, a prospect that raised a few nervous smiles in the royal houses of Europe.

Stalin once advised the Yugoslav dictator Josef 'Tito' Broz to restore the King of Yugoslavia to the throne. Tito was bemused, but then Stalin reminded him: "Don't worry, you can always stick a knife in his back when no one's looking."

Although Stalin and Tito were allies during World War II, Tito grew tired of being pushed around by Moscow and relations deteriorated to the point where the two leaders hated each other.

To make his point, Stalin arranged several assassination attempts on his former ally, none of which succeeded. Eventually Tito responded by writing a letter to Stalin: it read "Stop sending people to kill me. If you don't stop sending killers, I'll send one to Moscow, and I won't have to send a second."

Stalin kept the letter on his desk as a reminder and kept on dreaming up new ways of assassinating Tito, with plans ranging from plague-soaked tuxedos to sniper rifles that emit tear gas, right up until the Soviet leader's death in 1953. Tito outlived him by 27 years.

Blind faith

Joaquin Balaguer, the diminutive President of the Dominican Republic, wore black suits, black hats and black ties every day for nineteen years after his mother died in 1973. He never married and was said to lead the austere life of a deeply religious bachelor. His critics however pointed out that the dictator fathered seven illegitimate children by two dwarfs he employed as housemaids.

Balaguer kept the reins of power for twenty-two years through a combination of bribery and blatant ballot-box fraud. The self-styled 'Dominican Nazarene' toured the countryside in a Popemobile-type vehicle with a glass tower, handing out gifts to peasants, ranging from sweets and bicycles to money and plots of land; during his 1994 election campaign he tried to woo female supporters by handing out red panties.

He was re-elected six times, the last three when he was almost completely blind, with the slogan, 'I will not be asked to thread needles while in office'. In 1996, blind, deaf and eighty-nine years old, Balaguer challenged a civil servant suspected of fraud to a duel, but changed his mind at the last minute and settled for a speech in parliament instead.

Balaguer bankrupted his country by spending millions on a massive illuminated cross, intended to commemorate the 500th anniversary of the arrival of Christopher Columbus in the Americas. Slums were razed to make way for the project and escalating costs led to soaring food prices but he canceled the opening ceremony after being snubbed by his invited guests, the King of Spain and the Pope.

When the illumination was finally switched on for the first time it caused a massive and disastrous drain on the national grid, unnoticed however by the 60 per cent of his people who still did not have electricity.

Papa Doc's prayer

'Papa Doc' Duvalier liked to terrorize the uneducated peasantry of Haiti by posing as the incarnation of a malevolent voodoo deity called Baron Samedi, guardian of the graveyard, but liked to keep all bases covered by comparing himself to Jesus Christ. His best-known propaganda image showed a picture of him sitting down with Christ standing behind, his right hand on the president's shoulder, with the legend, 'I have chosen him'. A permanently flashing neon sign outside the presidential palace meanwhile proclaimed: 'I am the Haitian flag: I am indivisible'.

He also had the Lord's Prayer rewritten for use in Haitian schools: 'Our Doc, who art in the National Palace for life, hallowed be Thy name by present and future generations. Thy will be done in Port-au-Prince as it is in the provinces. Give us this day our new Haiti, and forgive not the trespasses of those anti-patriots who daily spit upon our country . . .'.

The Reich stuff

Alexander Lukashenko became president of Belarus in 1994. The event passed largely unremarked in the west, until a year later when a hot air balloon involved in a competition drifted into Belarusian airspace and the president had it shot down, killing the American pilot.

Lukashenko had more in common with his idols Hitler and Stalin than fancy facial hair. Although a quarter of his countrymen died during the German occupation, Lukashenko confessed to being a huge admirer of Hitler's leadership qualities. When swift international condemnation followed, he backed down and admitted that the Nazis were 'bad on foreign policy'.

In 1997 a Belarus TV director made a documentary poking fun at his country's eccentric leader. *An Ordinary President* was shown on television in Germany and France and although officially banned in Belarus about 140,000 copies were made and distributed throughout the country. Two days after the program went out, the TV director responsible answered his doorbell and was greeted by two men, who broke his legs.

Freeze frame

Macias Nguema President of Equatorial Guinea underwent several confusing changes of title. By the end of his rule he was known as Unique Miracle and Grand Master of Education, Science and Culture.

Nguema was prone to making rash pronouncements while under the influence of *iboga*, a local hallucinogen with effects similar to LSD.

In one speech he described Adolf Hitler as "the saviour of Africa" and ordered workers at the power plant of Malabo, the capital city, to stop using lubricating oil to save money; he promised he would keep the machinery going with magic. The plant exploded, plunging the capital into darkness.

In 1974 Nguema ordered all of his country's Catholic priests to hang a framed portrait of their head of state on the church altar, above the message: 'Only and unceasing miracle of Equatorial Guinea. God created Equatorial Guinea thanks to Macias. Without Macias, Equatorial Guinea would not exist.' A priest who refused to cooperate was later found frozen to death in a refrigeration truck.

A blossoming cult

Over a two year period from 1992 the North Korean authorities published over 300 poems and over 400 hymns in praise of their Dear Leader Kim Jong-Il.

Many paid tribute to Kim's skills as a cutting-edge gardener. He is said to have grown and nurtured a new flower, a hybrid orchid called *Kimjongilia*. According to the North Korean press, on Kim's birthday *Kimjongilia* has been known to miraculously bloom in the dead of winter.

I Don't Like Bash Guns

The people of Turkmenistan were required to swear an oath of loyalty to President Saparmurat Niyazov with the line: 'If I criticize you, may my tongue fall out'. Their chief executive alternated totalitarian ruthlessness and arbitrary oppression with token acts of kindness - stopping his motorcade to distribute cash to children or randomly pardoning criminals, for example. In 1993 he jailed his few remaining political opponents, but then abolished the death penalty and issued a blanket political amnesty after a bout with kidney disease caused a rethink. Niyazov explained: 'I had a bad dream about the death penalty. I think I was killing innocent people, so I'm not doing that any more.'

Having already raised expectations by abolishing ballet, theatre, circuses, loud mobile-phone conversations, music in cars, maths tuition in schools, gold teeth (people who already had gold teeth had them extracted) makeup on female newscasters, beards and long hair on men, in 2002 Niyazov showed he still had a few surprises up his sleeve - by abolishing the calendar.

Days of the week were renamed to *Bash Gun* (Main Day), *Yash Gun* (Young Day), *Hosh Gun* (Good Day), *Sogap Gun* (Blessed Day), *Anna* (Friday), *Rukh Gun* (Spiritual Day) and *Dynch Gun* (Rest Day). Months of the year were renamed after his country's heroes and most potent national symbols; thus January became Turkmenbashi (after himself) and April became simply Mother, after his dearly departed mum.

He also issued a decree redefining youth and age. All Turkmen up to the age of twenty-five are officially 'adolescents'. People between the ages of twenty-five and thirty-seven are in their 'youth'; from forty-nine to sixty-one, 'prophetic'. The ages between sixty-two and seventy-three belong to the 'inspirational'.

'Old age' is conveniently postponed to eighty-five - another twenty-three years before Turkmen have to fret about retirement. People between the ages of ninety-seven and one hundred and nine are designated *Oguzkhan*, after the supposed father of the Turkmen nation. There is no word for those who outlive the system. The life expectancy for the average Turkmen male is sixty years.

War trophy

From the day it became a republic in 1823 to the 'coronation' of the dictator Porfirio Diaz in 1876, Mexico had seventy-four different governments in fifty-three years, a perilous and unpredictable period when a show of firearms could make just about anyone president for a day. One Mexican chief executive, Victoriano Huerta, shot a man dead on the floor of the Mexican Senate for making a speech against him.

One of the few presidents who did not succumb to a fatal dose of lead poisoning was the toughest of the tough, the hero of the Alamo, Antonio Lopez de Santa Anna. Surviving defeats, sex scandals, opium addiction and well-founded accusations of corruption, Santa Anna served as president of his country eleven times and lived to die in his bed at the age of eighty-two.

Santa Anna and his troops were once stationed near a wood known to be full of Texan soldiers, but as it was after mid-day they insisted on taking their usual siesta. While Santa Anna and his men quietly snoozed, the Texans attacked and routed the entire Mexican army in less than twenty minutes. Santa Anna escaped, but two years later had a leg torn off in a skirmish with the French. He recovered the severed leg and when he eventually became the most powerful man in Mexico, he gave the limb a full state funeral. At public events he took to riding on horseback waving his new cork leg over his head as a symbol of his sacrifices for his country.

In 1847, at the Battle of Cerro Gordo in Mexico, Santa Anna was again caught flat-footed while enjoying a quiet roast chicken lunch when his appetite was ruined by an uninvited regiment of Illinoisans, who rudely stole his cork leg. Santa

Anna hopped away to fight another day, but the iconic limb remained in American hands, despite many requests from the Mexican government to return it. In the 1850's army veterans charged a nickel or a dime for curiosity-seekers to handle the leg in hotel bars.

Santa Anna's prosthesis currently resides in the Guard's Museum, Camp Lincoln in Springfield, Illinois, and in 2014 became the subject of a dispute with the Texan the San Jacinto Battle Monument, who launched a petition on the White House website, hoping to get 100,000 signatures to lure an important artifact back to Texas.

Space cadet

The Buddhist billionaire businessman Kirsan Ilyumzhinov was elected president of the tiny former Soviet republic of Kalmykia in 1993 after promising voters $100 each and 'a mobile phone for every shepherd'.

Despite pledges that he would turn the one party state into a prosperous country (the second Kuwait) and that passenger jets would soon be taking off from the Kalmyk airport, it mysteriously failed to become an international hub. Local pilots were unemployed because there wasn't any fuel, drinking water had to be imported by truck from neighbouring states and even the number of sheep fell. The only obvious sign of advancement was their billionaire president's growing collection of Rolls Royces.

After meeting the Pope in 1993, Ilyumzhinov pledged to spend millions building a Catholic church. When he returned home he was told that there was only one Catholic in Buddhist Kalmykia, but he went ahead and built the church anyway.

Ilyumzhinov claims telepathic powers, an advantage that did not however come in useful when he was abducted by aliens in 2001. "I have been on a UFO," he announced to the press. He explained; "The extraterrestrials put a yellow space suit on me. They gave me a tour of the spaceship and showed me the command centre. I felt very comfortable with it".

Forbidden fruit

Mangoes assumed a very important and symbolic role in China's Cultural Revolution.

In 1968 Chairman Mao received a delegation from Pakistan headed by the foreign minister and was presented with a basket of them. The Great Helmsman wasn't personally keen on mangoes, however, and decided to give them away.

Each of the seven pieces of fruit was presented to one of the many Worker-Peasant Mao Zedong Thought Propaganda Teams that were active in Peking and had been set up to keep an eye on the Red Guards. In reality, the gift of the fruit indicated Mao's displeasure with the Red Guards and his support for the Thought Propaganda Teams. The recipients of the mangoes were overjoyed at this 'Great, Greatest, Happiest of Events'; newspapers and official posters were filled with mango mania.

There were however no reports of anyone actually eating the fruit. Even though most Chinese people were starving, the artifacts were of far too important to eat: besides, nobody would have been worthy of this privilege but Mao himself.

Some of the recipients became obsessed with preserving their gift. In one case, the mango was mounted in a small glass case, engraved with an inscription and an image of Mao with shafts of light radiating from his head. Another mango was placed in a huge tank of water in a factory; each employee was given a small amount of the water to drink and to be literally filled with the spirit of Mao forever.

The Peking People's Printing Agency injected their mango with formaldehyde to preserve it for all eternity. It was to no avail: like Mao himself, this mango eventually turned black and shriveled.

Facing the music

Manuel Noriega, president of Panama, was the iron fist behind his country's former leader Omar Torrijos. With the backing of his country's cocaine lobby, he took control when his boss was killed in a plane crash in 1981.

Eight years later, the US invaded Panama and arrested Noriega on charges of drug trafficking, money laundering and racketeering - the first foreign head of state ever to face criminal charges in a US law court.

During the American invasion the ousted dictator took refuge in the Vatican embassy. US troops tried to flush him out by playing AC/DC's *Highway to Hell* at maximum volume. AC/DC front man Brian Johnson, reflecting on this misuse of his band's oeuvre noted, "I guess now we won't get to play for the Pope."

The Italian journalist Riccardo Orizio wrote a book *Talk of the Devil: Encounters with Seven Dictators*, in which he interviewed several former despots and wives of late despots, including Idi Amin, Jean-Bédel Bokassa, Nexhmije Hoxha (wife of Enver), Jean-Claude 'Baby Doc' Duvalier and Mengistu Haile Mariam. There should have been eight. Noriega, serving time in a Florida prison since 1992, declined to be interviewed. The indignant former despot wrote a letter to Orizio complaining that he did not yet belong in the category of 'forgotten dictators', adding "God has not yet written the last word on Manuel A. Noriega".

All clapped out

At the end of a Soviet Communist party rally in 1938, the traditional tribute to Comrade Stalin was called for. Everyone leaped to their feet and the hall rang out to a great ovation. After five minutes of deafening applause some of the older party members began to wilt. After a couple more minutes, even Stalin's most diehard supporters wondered if the clapping would ever stop, but no one dared be the first to quit. Certainly not the new local District Party secretary who had called for the ovation, having just taken the place of a man who had been arrested. Besides, Stalin's secret police were always watching. Finally, after eleven minutes, to massive relief all around, the director of a local paper factory sat down, and everyone else followed. Later that night the factory director was arrested. After signing a 'confession' his interrogators advised him: "don't be the first to stop applauding ever again".

Mao's visitors

Chairman Mao Zedong outstripped Stalin and Hitler combined as a homicidal maniac with an estimated total of 70 million dead from deliberate starvation during his Great Leap Forward and the Cultural Revolution - now officially classified as 'mistakes', committed when Mao was old and no longer in control of his faculties.

Mao showed signs that he might be losing his grip when US President Richard Nixon made a trip to China in the early 1970's. Nixon was quite surprised to be informed by the elderly communist leader, "I voted for you at your last election".

During trade talks in Beijing in 1973, Chairman Mao made what the US Secretary of State Henry Kissinger called "a novel proposition". Mao told him: "You know, China is a very poor country. We don't have much. What we have in excess is women. So if you want them we can give a few of those to you, some tens of thousands.' A few minutes later, Mao upped the offer: 'We can give you 10 million.' Kissinger replied "We will have to study it."

Although he had lost the election of 1974 and was no longer British Prime Minister, Edward Heath continued to trade on his status as world statesmen, especially in China where he had always been held in high esteem.

Soon after his defeat he had a meeting with Mao, a cordial exchange conducted via an interpreter, Prime Minister Chou En Lai.

After an initial exchange of pleasantries, a puzzled Chairman Mao demanded to know why Heath had not been greeted with full state honours when he arrived in Peking. Chou En Lai explained that Heath was no longer leader of his country.

"What did he say?" Heath enquired.

"He asked who is now the leader of your country." Chou En Lai replied.

"Mr. Wilson," answered Heath.

Mao spoke again.

"What did he say?" Heath enquired.

"He said, may Mr. Wilson stew in eternal shit."

☠ The Little Book of Loony Dictators ☭

PROFILE: SADDAM HUSSEIN

Born: at Al-Tikriti on 28 April 1947

Died: 30 December 2006

Also known as: Great Uncle; Anointed One; Glorious Leader; Direct Descendant of the Prophet; The World's Most Evil Man (courtesy of George W. Bush)

Occupation: President of Iraq, Chairman of Iraqi Revolutionary Command Council 1979 - 2003; full title His Excellency, President Saddam Hussein, Servant of God, Believer, Leader of All Muslims

Hobbies: a keen fisherman, but with little time for the subtleties of angling; preferred to lob hand grenades into the water then have a diver pick up the dead fish

Career highlights: (1) to celebrate his 'victory' in the first Gulf War - the Mother of All Battles - he commissioned a court calligrapher to reproduce a copy of Islam's holy book, the Koran, written entirely with Saddam's blood. The book is 605 pages long and took three years and fifty pints of blood, donated at a pint a time (2) the theme tune for his 2002 campaign for 're-election' as president of Iraq was Whitney Houston's *I Will Always Love You*

Career lowlights: as a daring young Ba'ath party activist attempted to shoot the Iraqi prime minister Abdul Kareem Qassem but missed and shot himself in the foot; (2) the French magazine *Le Nouvel Observateur* published an article calling Saddam "a monster, an executioner, a complete cretin and a noodle." Saddam sued for libel and lost

Style: dressed to kill and often did. Crimes against interior design

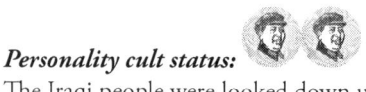

Personality cult status:
The Iraqi people were looked down upon constantly by thousands of giant Saddam portraits; in the countryside he was depicted as a farmer, in the factory as a laborer, in the barracks he wore military fatigues. Baath Party commissars however struggled when asked to portray their leader in Baghdad's newly opened showpiece gynecology clinic

Whimsical cruelty factor:
When he wasn't murdering the population with poison gas, punishments dished out followed a meticulously calibrated scale of barbarity. Deserters had an ear cut off. Thieves had fingers or hands cut off, depending on the source and value of stolen goods. Liars had their backs broken; offenders were tied facedown on a wooden plank between two cement blocks and another block was dropped on the victim's spine. Informants who supplied the state police with tips that proved false had a piece of red-hot iron placed on their tongue. Homosexuals were often bound then pushed off the roof of a building. Traitors, spies, smugglers and occasionally prostitutes paid the ultimate price - beheading with a 5-foot broadsword known as al-Bashar.

PROFILE: KIM JONG-IL

Born: 16 February 1941, his birth having been foretold by a swallow from heaven and attended by a bright star and double rainbows

Also known as: Dear Leader: Unprecedented Great Man; Bright Star of the Country; Guiding Focus; Genius of the Cinema; Shorty; the Asian Elvis

Occupation: Supreme Leader of North Korea 1997 - 2011

Hobbies: maintained a harem of around 2,000 imported blondes and young Asian women - the 'Joy Brigade' comprising a 'satisfaction team' for sexual favors, a 'happiness team' for massages and a 'dancing team' for post-coital karaoke and dancing performances. He was also believed to be Asia's biggest collector of pornography.

Career highlights: (1) according to Pyongyang media reports Kim has learned how to 'expand space and shrink time', a rare gift in a man who is afraid to fly or even board a plane. (2) in 2005 he ordered the men of North Korea to cut their hair. A TV campaign entitled 'let's trim our hair in accordance with the socialist lifestyle' warned men that long hair could sap their brains.

Significant others: (1) deceased father Kim Il-Sung who holds the post of 'Eternal Leader', but one of his many accomplishments; he once turned sand into rice and could cross rivers on a leaflet. Both Kims said to be descended from Tangun, a divine 'bear-man' who founded their country more than 5,000 years ago (2) son and

☠ The Little Book of Loony Dictators ☭

current North Korean leader Kim Jong-un.

Style: platform shoes, slick sunglasses and power romper suits

Personality cult status:
enjoyed a personality cult beyond Mao's wildest dreams, lauded as all round great soldier, peerless film-maker, movie critic, philosopher, scientist, brilliant and industrious scholar imbued with great wisdom etc. etc. His father Kim Il-sung has around seventy bronze statues and over 20,000 plaster busts made in his image. The entire population of North Korea was also compelled to wear lapel badges bearing the face of their Eternal Leader. There were twenty different kinds of badges to choose from, worn according to class.

Whimsical cruelty factor:
disloyalty to the memory of Kim Jong-Il's late father is punishable by torture and imprisonment. Offences include allowing pictures of the Eternal Leader to gather dust or be torn or folded.

CHAPTER FIVE
STAND BY YOUR MAO

'Til death do us part

Eva Braun, wife of Adolf Hitler, eventually married her boyfriend fifteen years after they first met, then celebrated by swallowing poison the following day; *der Führer* took his own life two minutes later.

Generally regarded as not the brightest of dictator's consorts, Eva dreamed of a post-war career as a film actress. The part she wanted to play was Hitler's lover in a big Hollywood movie. After Germany conquered the United States, presumably.

Eva was once asked to donate some of her fur coats to German soldiers who were freezing on the Russian front. She refused, on the grounds that she was sure the soldiers would not want such nice furs in a "dirty" place. "Besides", she said, "I need something nice to wear in the winter too". Her furs, about fifty in total, were put into storage and liberated by the US Army at the end of the war.

Cracked actress

Qing Jiang, 'Madame Mao', the Shanghai actress who became the fourth wife of Mao Zedong was one of China's most powerful and reviled figures and once described as 'the Yoko Ono of contemporary Chinese politics'.

She used her position to settle a few old personal scores. During the Cultural Revolution Madame Mao remembered that decades earlier, when she was a young actress, she had lost a part to a rival called Wang Ying. Madame Mao had her arrested and thrown into prison, where she died.

While brutalizing China's artists and intellectuals Madame Mao also had a soft spot for Western tearjerkers. One of the Cultural Revolution's victims, Shi Xianrong, a translator of Arthur Miller, was demoted to pig farming in the gulag.

One day he was summoned to appear before Madame Mao, where he discovered to his astonishment that his task was to be a private translation of Erich Segal's *Love Story* and *Jonathan Livingston Seagull* by Richard Bach.

The filler in Manila

Imelda, wife and confidante of the Philippine dictator Ferdinand Marcos, experienced a 'mystical vision', which prompted her to spend $100 million on a Philippine version of the Cannes film festival. Most of the money was spent on an extravagant new film theatre. The builders and everyone else associated with the Marcos family were so corrupt that no one was particularly surprised when, two months before the official opening in 1982, half of the building collapsed killing at least thirty workers. To avoid delaying construction she had concrete poured over the dead men and had the theatre exorcised to appease the superstitious.

The grand opening went ahead almost exactly as Imelda had planned, with just one minor setback: she had invited the Pope, but in the event had to settle for Brooke Shields.

Educating Elena

Before she became Romania's First Lady, Elena Ceausescu held a variety of unskilled jobs, including a brief spell as a hired hand in a back street laboratory producing dodgy slimming and headache pills. Her lab experience came in useful years later when her husband appointed her chairman of ICECHIM, the main chemistry research laboratory in Romania. Almost as mysteriously, she acquired a doctorate in chemistry, a remarkable achievement for one who left school with only a certificate in needlework, and a new official title. From now on she was to be known in all communications as 'Elena Ceausescu, world-renowned chemist and scientist'.

Most of her official trips abroad were excuses to acquire honorary degrees in recognition of her scientific work. The Romanian foreign office negotiated with the most distinguished academic institutions in whatever country the Ceausescus were planning to visit to seek awards for Elena, along with a hint that the couple might cancel their trip if an award was not forthcoming.

Before her official visit to Britain in 1978, Oxford and Cambridge universities and the Fellowship of the Royal Society were approached and asked if they would like to give Madame Ceausescu an honorary degree. The petitions were politely turned down. She was delighted however to receive honorary degrees from both Central London Polytechnic and the Royal Institute of Chemistry.

Elena was less impressed in 1978 when she went to the United States. As no Washington-based academy was prepared to aknowledge her scientific achievements, she was offered membership of the Illinois Academy of Science. She accepted the award grudgingly, noting that she had never heard of Illinois and was put out at having to accept such a 'low-ranked' degree from the hands of a 'dirty Jew'; she was referring to the brilliant chemist Dr. Emanuel Merdinger, the Jewish-American head of the Illinois Academy of Science, who had spent most of World War II in a Nazi concentration camp.

To keep up appearances as a 'brilliant scientist of world renown', the writings of many genuine Romanian scientists were often published under her name. She often complained that she had never been nominated for the Nobel Prize in chemistry, despite her many publications.

A hard day's night in Manila

Imelda Marcos had one of the rooms in her palace converted to a karaoke hall so she could lip-synch pop songs, but there were no Lennon/McCartney numbers in her repertoire.

In 1966 the Beatles went to play a concert in Manila and on a tight schedule and expecting a quick getaway, they politely declined an invitation to take tea with the First Lady. Furious at the snub, Imelda withdrew the security assigned to the Fab Four, leaving them at the mercy of thousands of hostile Philippines, protesting the perceived discourtesy, booing, kicking and jostling them as they left their hotel then plastering the band's get-away limousine all the way back to the airport. Later, Imelda enforced a ban on Beatles records in the Philippines, which lasted for many years.

Power programming

Female news presenters on Romanian TV were not allowed to wear jewelry in case they appeared more glamorous than their First Lady, Ceausescu. She also ordered a TV blackout after 10pm so that the workers of Romania could wake up early in the morning, fresh to start a new day's work in order to complete the five-year plan.

Her husband meanwhile banned Romania's three favourite TV programmes, all of them British imports; *The Avengers*, *The Forsyte Saga* and *The Saint*.

Toilet break

Because of her bloody role in the Cultural Revolution, Madame Mao became extremely paranoid and was terrified of sudden, loud noises. Her staff were warned to speak softly and never to cough, sneeze or wear shoes around her, on pain of certain imprisonment. They were also required to walk with their legs apart to prevent their clothes from rustling.

In a vain attempt to retain her looks and youthful vigour,

Madame Mao had regular blood transfusions from young men. Scores of her husband's Praetorian Guards were screened with rigorous health checks, and then four 'volunteers' were selected and placed on permanent stand-by as blood donors.

Despite her best efforts, Madame Mao could not hold back time. One night she was taken short and attempted to squat on a spittoon, having mistaken it for a commode. She fell off, breaking her collarbone. Madame Mao later insisted that the embarrassing incident had been part of an assassination plot.

I rest my case

Nigeria's military dictator Sani Abacha, who enjoyed hanging his critics while videotaping the executions for his personal viewing pleasure, stole more than $4 billion during his five-year reign.

Abacha died of a heart attack in 1998, aged 54, during a Viagra-fuelled romp with two, or possibly three prostitutes.

A few weeks after his death police at Kano airport became suspicious when his widow, Maryam, tried to leave the country with thirty-eight pieces of luggage; each was found to be stuffed with US dollars. Mrs. Abacha explained she was not stealing the money, just 'putting away the funds in some foreign accounts for safe keeping'.

Footnote

Imelda Marcos's influence as a world-class buyer of fashion footwear cannot be understated. In addition to the 1,060 pairs of shoes that the Philippine government eventually confiscated from Imelda, including the pair of simple canvas espadrilles she was wearing at the time she had to flee from the palace to escape a revolt, they also took her only bulletproof bra.

Big Daddy's First Ladies

Idi Amin fathered an estimated 43 children, mostly by his four wives, Sarah, Kay, Norah and Medina. A persistent suitor, Amin murdered the partners of women he liked the look of then consigned them to his fridge.

He met one of his four wives, Sarah Kyolaba Amin, known as Suicide Sarah, in 1974 when she was serving as a teenage dancer with his army's Revolutionary Suicide Mechanized Regiment Band; the head of her then fiancé Jesse Gitta became one of many stored in the refrigerator of Amin's 'Botanical Room'. Idi and Sarah's wedding banquet in 1975 cost $3million and was attended by the best man, Palestinian leader Yasser Arafat - an interesting choice, at the time regarded as an international pariah. Sarah left Amin in 1982 and sought political asylum in Germany, where she spent time as a lingerie model, then moved to London, running a café serving African dishes including goat stew and cow hoof in gravy.

In 1999 environmental health officers closed her down when they found a 'grey furry thing' in her kitchen. It was identified as a decomposing mouse.

Unluckily for all of wives, Amin suffered from tertiary syphilis. In 1974 he lectured students at Kampala's conference centre: "I am told venereal disease is very high with you. You had better go to hospital and make yourselves very clean, or you will infect the whole population."

Her indoors

Eva Peron, who was said to have kept a glass jar on her desk containing the genitals of some of her husband's political enemies, rose from obscurity to become the second wife of Argentine President Juan Domingo Peron and the First Lady of Argentina from 1946 until her death from uterine cancer in 1952, from at the age of thirty-three.

By the time of her death the Spanish pathologist Dr. Pedro Ara had been on stand-by for a fortnight to embalm her. Her husband planned to have her housed in a giant new mausoleum, but in 1955 he was forced to flee the country in a hurry. Eva's embalmed body was confiscated by the Argentinean military,

who feared that it would become a rallying point for Peronists.
For several years the corpse was moved from place to place; copies were even made out of wax, vinyl and fiberglass to throw Eva's followers off the trail. Her kidnapper Colonel Moori Koenig was known to display the body to his friends and to fondle it; Eva's sister later hinted at more sinister goings on, saying only, "there are some things that should not be spoken of". In 1971 Juan and Eva were touchingly reunited, although by now her nose was broken, a fingertip and one of her ears were missing and her feet were mysteriously coated in tar.
The corpse became ever-present in an open casket at the Peron family dinner table, even though Peron now had a new wife, Isabel, who liked to comb Eva's hair.

Lynch party

Eliza Alicia Lynch, the beautiful Irish mistress of the stubby-legged Paraguayan dictator Francisco Lopez, was variously known as 'Madame Lynch' and 'the Irish whore'.
While her husband was killing off 95% of the male population of Paraguay by waging a pointless war of attrition against his neighbors, Eliza bled the country dry in her quest for fairytale palaces, marble baths and extravagant banquets - a Josephine to the Napoleon of the South Americas.
As Paraguay's demoralized, ill-equipped and mostly starving soldiers awaited death she tried to raise morale by touring the army camps in a black coach, followed by several carriage-loads of her extensive wardrobe of Parisian gowns and a grand piano. At one point she appeared on a battlefield dressed in white crinolines.
When the war was lost, after burying her husband's body in a jungle grave, she fled the country, hastily abandoning the lands and jewels she had accrued. In 1961 Paraguay's notorious former 'First Lady' became the centre of international intrigue when a Lebanese drug dealer climbed over a wall and stole her remains from a Paris cemetery. The thief smuggled them

back to Paraguay where he hoped to curry favour with the country's new dictator, Alfredo Stroessner - although it generally believed that he took the wrong body.

Stroessner declared Eliza Lynch a national heroine and planned to have her laid to rest alongside her late lover in the Pantheon of Heroes. The Catholic Church stopped Stroessner's plan: not because of her role in the blackest period of Paraguay's history, but because the couple had never married.

Her remains were left in a cupboard on the first floor of the ministry of defense for almost a decade, until 1970 - the one hundredth anniversary of Paraguay's disastrous War of the Triple Alliance - when they were interred in a huge new marble mausoleum.

Today a plaque over her urn in Paraguay's Madame Lynch Museum proclaims the courage of the woman '"who selflessly accompanied the greatest hero of the nation, Marshal Francisco Solano Lopez."

Family affair

Romania's First Lady Elena Ceausescu employed her husband's secret police to film the sexual liaisons of foreign diplomats and used the evidence for blackmail. She abandoned the practice when her daughter Zoia showed up on one of the tapes.

King Congo

President Mobutu of Zaire slept with a bottle of patent medicine by his bedside for "rheumatism and syphilis". He also slept with the wives of his government ministers and officials, both to humiliate his underlings and "to keep an eye on things".

After the death of his first wife, Marie Antoinette, Mobutu married his mistress, Boby, with whom he already had several children, then took her identical twin sister, Kossia, as his new mistress. No one could tell them apart, except possibly Mobutu. He said he kept twins as lovers to ward off malignant influences from his first wife's spirit.

Plain speaking

After her husband's death in exile, in 1991 Imelda Marcos made a triumphant return to the Philippines, corruption charges notwithstanding. When asked if she had any intention of returning the suspected eight billion dollars stolen from the national treasury, she responded in the negative: "If you give it back, it means you've stolen it."

She went on to justify her notorious extravagance by revealing a previously unknown and medical condition: "I am allergic to ugliness."

* * *

Chairman Mao was once asked what would have happened if Khrushchev had been assassinated instead of President Kennedy in 1963.

"Well, I'll tell you one thing" said Mao, "Aristotle Onassis wouldn't have married Mrs. Khrushchev."

PROFILE: ALEXANDER LUKASHENKO

Born: 30 August 1954

Also known as: Father Luke, 'the last dictator in Europe'.

Occupation: President of Belarus 1994 - 2011

Hobbies: ice hockey and roller-skating - regularly took part in televised ice-hockey games in which he strode past defenders with dictatorial ease and once closed a main highway in Minsk so he could roller-skate in private. Also took a very keen personal interest in state-sponsored beauty contests

Career highlights: (1) swept to power in 1994 with the campaign slogan: 'You will live badly, but not for long' (2) admitting rigging the 2006 election, in which official results showed he received 83% of the vote. He revealed later that he actually got 93%, but ordered it to be revised down because it looked 'a bit over the top'.

Career lowlight: in 2005 extended a warm welcome to foreign asylum-seekers, provided they were prepared to live in Chernobyl

Significant others: estranged wife Galina; various mistresses including singer Irina Dorofeyeva, Miss Belarus Lika Yalinskaya and personal physician Irina Abelskaya, allegedly the mother of his illegitimate son

Style: Stalin with a comb-over, dressed his six year old son in military uniforms

Personality cult status:
In the many state shops you will find at least one or two portraits of the proudly combed-over President.

Whimsical cruelty factor:
like his idols Stalin and Hitler, became famous for his death squads - executed convicts with a shot to the back of the head. In 1999 three opposition figures and a journalist disappeared after Lukashenko promised to crack down on 'opposition scum'. Troublesome journalists vanished or were found mysteriously knifed to death by persons unknown. Once sentenced a 16-year-old boy to 18 months hard labour for defacing a statue of Lenin.

PROFILE: FERDINAND MARCOS

Born: 11 September 1917

Died: 28 September 1989

Occupation: President of the Republic of the Philippines 1965 - 1986.

Hobbies: pocketing generous handouts from the World Bank

Career highlight: political career got off to a flying start at the age of twenty-one when he shot his father's victorious opponent in the Philippines' elections. Subsequently elected President of the Philippines in 1965, despite his record as a murderer and a Nazi sympathizer

Career lowlight: repeated his party trick in 1983 when exiled chief opposition leader Benigno Aquino returned to the Philippines; Aquino was shot in the head as he stepped out to the tarmac at Manila International Airport in front of a planeload of journalists

Significant others: former beauty queen wife Imelda (Miss Manila 1958), so high maintenance that according to a US Senator she "made Marie Antoinette look like a bag lady"

Style: according to his diaries he thought of himself as combining the best qualities of Napoleon and Julius Caesar

Personality cult status:
monumental vanity. He had his face carved into a mountainside, *á la* Mount Rushmore

Whimsical cruelty factor:
had his enemies' heads slammed into walls and their genitals and pubic hair torched.

CHAPTER SIX
DICTATOR-LIT: THE DESPOTIC MUSE

Mein iPad

Adolf Hitler wrote his autobiography to cash in on the publicity stirred up by his trial and imprisonment for his part in the Beer Hall Putsch in 1924. Originally titled *Four And A Half Years of Struggle Against Lies, Stupidity and Cowardice*, the first publisher he contacted turned it down flat, dismissing it as a badly written and rambling collection of "banalities, schoolboy reminiscences, subjective judgments and personal hatred".

A friend of Adolf's suggested he change the title to the pithier *Mein Kampf* and it went on to become a runaway best-seller, translated into sixteen languages, earning its author millions from royalties. Thoughtfully, there was also a Braille version for the blind.

As the best selling western author of the twentieth century, Hitler died filthy rich on his royalties from *Mein Kampf*. His personal copy, bound in white calf, was looted by General Patton and presented to the Huntington Library in California, but was never actually put on display as the library feared that Hitler's birthday could attract annual pilgrimages of skinhead neo-Nazis.

In 2005 a signed copy of *Mein Kampf* fetched £23,800 at auction. The anonymous buyer was rumoured to be Queen Elizabeth II's husband Prince Philip, the Duke of Edinburgh, who was once thought to have owned one of the world's biggest collections of editions of the book.

In 2014 a digital edition of *Mein Kampf* topped the UK ebook charts. According to an industry commentator, the newfound popularity of Hitler's tract was down to the fact that it can now be consumed "in the privacy of our own iPads".

Tedious tyrant

The published transcripts of Enver Hoxha's speeches ran to thirty-nine volumes. Although infamously long-winded, they were seldom lacking in candour.

The president began his keynote New Year message to the Albanian people in 1967; "This year will be harder than last year. It will however be easier than next year."

Musso's muse

Benito Mussolini published forty-four books in and out of office, including his bodice-ripper *The Cardinal's Mistress.* Dorothy Parker once reviewed one of his novels: "This is not a book to be cast aside lightly. It should be hurled with great force."

Captive readership

Mao Zedong's 'little red book' *Quotations from Chairman Mao*, a collection of tips on such diverse subjects as farming, women and the need to keep up with your grenade-throwing practice, is one of the world's all-time best-sellers, with the estimated number in print exceeding one billion copies, ranking second only to the Bible.

Every Chinese citizen was required to carry as copy with him or her at all times. The punishment for failing to produce the book on demand ranged from a beating on the spot by Red Guards, to several years hard labour.

Study sessions with Chairman Mao's book were reputed to have miraculous restorative powers. Reading the book supplied the breath of life to soldiers gasping in the thin air of the Tibetan plateau, enabled workers to raise the sinking city of Shanghai three-quarters of an inch, inspired a million people to subdue a tidal wave in 1969, enabled inaccurate meteorologists to forecast weather correctly, caused a group of housewives to re-invent shoe polish and allowed surgeons to sew back severed fingers and remove a ninety-nine pound tumour as big as a football.

While he was busy executing capitalists, thanks to the royalties amassed from his writings, Chairman Mao enjoyed an executive lifestyle few billionaires could dream of. He cornered the Chinese literature market by the simple expedient of preventing the vast majority of authors from being published, making him the only self-made millionaire in Maoist China.

Essential reading

'Papa Doc' Duvalier wanted to be recognized as a great writer on a par with political theorists such as Marx, Trotsky and Mao. In 1967 the Haitian dictator published his Essential Works, an imitation of Mao's little red book right down to the red cover. Disappointed by poor sales, Papa Doc deducted $15 from the salary of all of Haiti's civil servants; in return the workers each received a copy of his book.

Hitler's blue period

Adolf Hitler's early ambition to become an artist was thwarted by two rejections from the Viennese Academy of Fine Arts when his drawing skills were declared "unsatisfactory." He blamed it on the Jewish members of the review board, not lack of talent. Later Adolf pinned his hopes on working on sets for the Vienna Court Opera's productions of Wagner with the renowned graphic artist and stage designer Alfred Roller. Carrying a letter of introduction, Hitler approached Roller's door three times, but could never pluck up the nerve to knock. Hitler's' taste in art was prosaic; "Anyone who sees and paints a sky green and fields blue", he said, "ought to be sterilized."

Dic-lit

In 1975 the Libyan leader Muammar Gaddafi wrote *The Green Book*, a work of political theory proffering his views on a wide range of subjects from breast feeding to "why the black race will prevail". A western critic reviewed it as "the sort of thing a fifteen year old might write under the title 'My plan to reform the world".

Gaddafi also tried his hand at writing fiction in *Escape to Hell*, a collection of short stories and essays. One tale tells of an astronaut who returns to earth and kills himself because he can't find a job. Another article discusses whether death is male or female. The introduction, supplied by Pierre Salinger, press secretary to the late President Kennedy, describes the book as "fascinating – the work of an original mentality."

Novel inspiration

Macias Nguema, president of Equatorial Guinea, failed his country's civil service exam three times. He developed an inferiority complex that turned to a hatred of intellectuals; he banned use of the word 'intellectual' and murdered anyone he found wearing spectacles; short sight was proof of intelligence and having read too much.

Ironically, Nguema was the unwitting inspiration for a popular classic. In 1970 *The Times* reported that the novelist Frederick Forsyth had put up a quarter of a million dollars to fund a coup against Nguema, employing twelve British mercenaries and fifty soldiers from Biafra. The 'plot' was blown when one of the mercenaries shot himself after a gunfight with London police. Forsyth denied any participation in the plot and said he was only researching a book; the resulting 'fictional' work, *The Dogs of War*, was a best seller.

Censorship by hostage

In 1973 the French film director Barbet Schroeder persuaded Idi Amin to star in a documentary, *General Idi Amin Dada: A Self Portrait.* Schroeder was attracted to his subject by news reports that Amin was sending random telegrams to world leaders: he sent several to Queen Elizabeth addressing her as 'Liz' and one to Richard Nixon wishing him a 'speedy recovery' from Watergate. Another Amin telegram sent to UN Secretary General Kurt Waldheim in 1972 noted, 'Hitler was right about the Jews'.

One of the highlights of the Schroeder documentary was a cabinet meeting during which Amin dictated policy while his ministers slavishly copied down his every word. For example; "Anybody found is a spy, his case must be dealt with by military tribunal. Even military tribunal should not waste time of making law all day discussing about one person who is a spy. Must be shortcut!" Amin also laid down rules, including: "Miss three meetings and you're kicked out of government".

Big Daddy was not happy with Schroeder's finished documentary and sought a solution to the problem in a suitably tyrannical fashion He rounded up every French citizen in Uganda, forced them into a hotel surrounded by armed military and threatened to kill then unless the director trimmed two minutes and twenty-one seconds from it. Schroeder made the requested cuts but restored the footage six years later when Amin was exiled.

The producer from hell

North Korea's Dear Leader Kim Jong-Il maintained a close personal interest in the film industry and once wrote a book on the subject: *Cinema and the Art of Directing*. The Pyongyang studio had regular visits from Kim, who issued artistic tips, displayed on huge billboards. These tips range from the general to the specific. One note read, 'make more cartoons'. In others, he tells actors how to laugh, how to cry, and how to be good citizens at home. An actor who is going to play a football player, Kim explained, "should actually become a football player himself and run sweating across the pitch to kick the ball."

When he finally met his favourite actress Choe Eun-hui, he asked her; "Well, Madame Choe, what do you think of my physique? Small as a midget's turd, aren't I?"

Kim Jong-Il had a long held ambition to make a Korean version of *Godzilla*. To realize his vision, in 1978 he kidnapped a noted South Korean film producer Shin Sang-ok and his wife, the actress Choe Eun-hui, so they could teach him how to make films. With the help of the reluctant director and his wife, Kim went on to make the epic *Pullgesari,* about a metal-eating monster that saves fourteenth century Korean peasants from the tyranny of an evil warlord. In 1998 when the film was seen outside the country for the first time it became an instant cult classic.

Tortured metaphors

Saddam Hussein liked to demonstrate his shy, sensitive side by penning anonymous romantic novels. Saddam wrote (or more likely, employed a team of professionals to ghost-write) two books; the first, *Zabibah and the King*, a patriotic parable about a benign despot who falls in love with a beautiful woman married to a brutish, vicious husband, became a best seller when published in 2000. One chapter describes the rape of the woman, which occurs on 17 January, coincidentally the day US and coalition forces launched the first Gulf War.

Saddam's second novel *The Fortified Castle*, published in 2001, didn't trouble the best-seller lists until Saddam's son Uday helpfully bought 250,000 copies. A third, unfinished work of fiction, provisionally titled *The Great Awakening*, was due for publication just before he was deposed.

Dear Reader

During his time at university Kim Jong-Il wrote 1,500 books inside three years.

He also found time to pen six full operas, "all of which are better than any in the history of music", according to his official biography.

PROFILE: JOSEPH MOBUTU

Born: 14 October 1930

Died: 7 September 1997

Also known as: the Big Man: the Leopard; the Messiah

Occupation: President of Zaire 1965 - 97 (regularly changed his official title from The Marshal to The Supreme Emperor to King of Zaire)

Hobbies: shopping - his garden had a runway big enough to take the Air France Concorde he regularly used to buy his groceries from Paris and Brussels.

Career highlight: theft of about $4billion in foreign aid

Career lowlight: during his visit to meet the Queen at Buckingham Palace in 1973, what was described in the press as "nearly a diplomatic incident" occurred when British customs officials refused to give a visa to Mobutu's pet terrier.

Significant others: first wife Marie- Antoinette, second wife Bobi and his mistress, Bobi's identical twin

Style: sharkskin suits, leopard-skin pillbox hats and Buddy Holly sunglasses

Personality cult status:
his portrait hung in every public building, depicted on television every day riding a cushion of clouds; government sources spun stories about his alleged supernatural feats, including the lion he killed with his bare hands at the age of seven and the battle he fought against Zaire's enemies in which bullets and spears bounced off his chest

Whimsical cruelty factor:
organized nightly helicopter flights to dump he bodies of his political opponents into the river Congo.

PROFILE: ROBERT MUGABE

Born: 21 February 1924

Also known as: Comrade Bob, the Teflon Tyrant

Occupation: Executive President of Zimbabwe 1980 -

Hobbies: home improvements - used government funds to build several luxury homes including a 30-bedroom mansion called Gracelands, in honor of his wife and her hero Elvis Presley

Career highlight: outed the entire British government in 1999 when he called them "the gangster gay government of the gay United gay Kingdom"

Career lowlight: awarded an honorary knighthood by Britain in 1994, nine years later the British government asked for the medal back

Significant others: former mistress and second wife Grace, 30 years his junior, known as Zimbabwe's First Shopper. She spent an estimated £200 million on jet fuel on foreign shopping sprees in a DC-9 airliner once owned by Playboy baron Hugh Hefner, spends more on a single shopping trip abroad than 90% of her compatriots earn in their lifetimes.

Style: millionaire, homophobic, racist Marxist. Reputed to be the most travelled head of state in the world, earning from his countrymen the nickname Vasco de Gama. A stickler for protocol, he berates ministers for not dressing properly and always arrives at Parliament in a Rolls Royce.

Personality cult status:
relatively low key. His portrait hangs in most business premises and every town has a street named after him, but there are no statues of him and his face does not appear on banknotes.

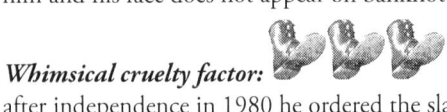

Whimsical cruelty factor:
after independence in 1980 he ordered the slaughter of 20,000 civilians in Matabeleland who supported his rival, Joshua Nkomo. He once boasted of having "degrees in violence" to go with his

seven academic degrees. Specialised in torture by electric shocks and clubbings organized by his right-hand man, Chenjerai Hunzvi, affectionately known as 'Hitler'. Locked up opponents for "discussing politics without a permit".

PROFILE: BENITO MUSSOLINI

Born: 29 July 1883

Died: 28 April 1945

Also known as: *Il Duce*; Musso the Wop

Occupation: Prime Minister of Italy 1922 - 43

Hobbies: fast sports cars, airplanes and an endless succession of mistresses

Career highlights: (1) invading Ethiopia (2) and Abyssinia (3) made the trains run on time

Career lowlight: strung upside down by piano wire in a Milanese square in April 1945

Significant others: wife Rachele, long-standing mistress Claretta Petacci

Style: eclectic; for his famous march on Rome (actually a train ride) he wore a bowler hat, starched collar, jodhpurs and white spats. He was also highly superstitious and refused to dine at a table if there were thirteen people present. He also liked to ward off the 'evil eye' by touching both of his testicles - an option not open to his fascist ally Adolf, who had only his right one.

Personality cult status:
his high-octane sex life an important part of the appeal of the Italian fascist movement; according to his propagandists, *Il Duce* thought pyjamas were 'effete' and always slept in his underwear

Whimsical cruelty factor:
the first 20th century despot to make torture official state policy; his

Blackshirts pumped their opponents full of castor oil to 'purge them of the will to live': victims usually choked to death.

Although a distant third on the scale of World War II dictators, he was responsible for the deaths of over 400,000 Italians and at least 30,000 Ethiopians.

CHAPTER SEVEN
SPORTING DICTATORS

In the hole [1]

According to the North Korean media, their Dear Leader Kim Jong-Il was the world's best ever golfer. Although he came to the sport late in 1994, on his very first outing at the brand new Pyongyang course he eagled the opening hole then went on to register eleven hole-in-ones on the way to shooting a 38 under par round. Satisfied with his performance, he immediately declared his retirement from the sport.

The previous lowest recorded score in PGA history was 59, attained only on three occasions by Al Geiberger (1977) Chip Beck (1991) and David Duval (1999).

Different ball game

Although he gained his country's presidency through the ballot box, by 1937 the Dominican leader Rafael Trujillo ruled as an iron-fisted dictator, in control of the army and placing family members into high political office. The only thing he did not yet control was baseball, his country's national obsession.

---

[1] The phrase in North Korea does not carry quite the same meaning as at Pebble Beach. A former North Korean football coach who defected in 2004 reported that under-performing players were sent to work coalmines if they lost.

Trujillo decided to form his own baseball team – the greatest team ever assembled - then dedicated the national baseball league to his re-election. There was more than sporting pride at stake. As his political opponents already owned a share in two other major teams in the Dominican League, for the dictator not to have the best baseball team in the country would have been an unacceptable loss of face.

Trujillo took over two of the existing biggest rival teams and merged them to form one squad, the Ciudad Trujillo Dragons, then improved it by raiding the black American leagues for their most talented players.

The climax of a tense season came when Trujillo's all-star side were forced into a dramatic seventh and deciding game of the championship series against a Cuban side, Estrellas de Oriente. On the eve of the big game Trujillo tipped the odds in his favour by having some of the opposition squad thrown into jail, then hinted to his own all-star team that their lives depended on a favourable result. When Trujillo's team entered the stadium the next day they found their employer's troops lined up with rifles and bayonets near the first-base. The Dragons took the hint, won the series and Trujillo was comfortably re-elected by his baseball-mad countrymen.

Despite winning the championship, Trujillo was not impressed with the return on his $30,000 investment, as the team didn't go on to dominate as he had anticipated. The following season the team and league was disbanded and here would not be organized baseball in the Dominican Republic for the next 12 years.

Trujillo wasn't the only Latin-American dictator to identify baseball with national pride. The Nicaraguan leader Anastasio Somoza once fired his national team manager in the middle of a game in disgust and went into the dugout to direct operations personally.

Fighting talk

Idi Amin was heavyweight boxing champion of Uganda from 1951-1960. When his country was being overrun by Tanzanian troops in 1978, he suggested that he and Tanzanian president Julius Nyere settle the war between them in the ring with Mohammed Ali as referee.
Amin was also a skilled rugby player and swimmer: he once phoned the Egyptian President Anwar Sadat to tell him that he was going to become the world's first head of state to swim across the Suez Canal. Amin also organized basketball games in which he alone was allowed to score. He once had a palace guard killed for blocking his shot.

Ping-pong diplomacy

In 1971 Chairman Mao allowed a team to go to Japan to compete in the World Table Tennis Championships, the first Chinese sportsmen to be allowed to travel abroad since the Cultural Revolution four years earlier.
They were given precise instructions on how to behave: they were not to fraternize with Americans, or shake their hands. To give them an even chance of winning, however, Mao rescinded an order requiring them brandish his 'little red book' during actual play.

Top seed

Benito Mussolini liked to show off his physical fitness by jogging down the lines when he was reviewing his troops. He also enjoyed humiliating out-of-shape visitors by making them run to his desk in the Palazzo Venezia and then run out again at the double, before saluting him from the door.
Il Duce was an enthusiastic but poor tennis player, which presented problems for his opponents.
The Italian foreign minister Count Galeazzo Ciano noted that it took more skill and stamina to lose to Mussolini than it did

to defeat most men.

His Axis ally Adolf Hitler, on the other hand, by his own Aryan ideals was puny and not at all athletic. Unlike Mussolini, who loved to pose topless, *der Führer h*ated being seen without his clothes on, even by his valet, and never wore shorts because he was ashamed of his white knees. Whenever Hitler went for a walk at his favourite Bavarian retreat it was only ever downhill and there was always a car at the bottom waiting to take him back up.

Ceausescu's flying bears

Nicolae Ceausescu loved hunting, but was a poor shot and nearly always bagged less than anyone else in his shooting party. To compensate, his aides brought supplies of dead game and hung it outside his hunting lodge.

Ceausescu mostly enjoyed shooting bears. Teams of forest rangers would spend hours preparing an area for a bear hunt, tying down half of a dead horse near a watering hole. When a large hungry bear arrived on the scene, the rangers would notify their president. Ceausescu would arrive by helicopter and depart with a bearskin a couple of hours later.

One day Ceausescu took aim, then fell over backwards when the bear, which had not been inadequately sedated, reared on its hind legs as if to attack. His shot flew harmlessly into the treetops: meanwhile three bullets entered the bear's heart, fired by snipers who were on hand to guarantee the dictator's marksmanship. Ceausescu didn't acknowledge the applause of his retainers.

Ceausescu also gave Romanian bears as gifts to cement relationships with neighbouring communist countries, such as Bulgaria. The bears were sent in military planes and released in the wild order to spice up the less impressive local bear population.

Curve ball

In 1956 Chairman Mao's Physical Culture and Sports Commission gave official recognition to a new track and field event, the hand-grenade throw.

Paying the penalty

Saddam Hussein appointed his son Uday as head of both Iraq's Olympic committee and the Iraqi soccer federation. It was an inspired choice designed to give his nation's top athletes an extra incentive to do well; under-performance was rewarded with beatings with iron bars or canings on the soles of feet, followed by dunkings in raw sewage to ensure the wounds became infected.

Motivational team talks included threats to cut off players' legs and throw them to ravenous dogs; a missed training session was punishable by imprisonment; a loss or a draw brought flogging with electric cable, or a bath in raw sewage. A penalty miss carried the certainty of imprisonment and torture. Players had their feet scalded and toenails ripped off.

During a World Cup qualifying match in Jordan, Iraq drew 3-3 with the United Arab Emirates, calling for a penalty shoot-out, which Iraq lost. Two days after the team returned to Baghdad the captain Zair was summoned to Uday's headquarters, blindfolded and taken away to a prison camp for three weeks.

Punishments for acquiring a red card were particularly harsh. Yasser Abdul Latif, accused of thumping the referee during a heated club match in Baghdad, was confined to a tiny prison cell, where he was stripped to the waist, then ordered to perform press-ups for two hours while guards flogged him with lengths of electric cable.

When Iraq lost 4–1 to Japan in the Asian Cup, goalkeeper Hashim Hassan, defender Abdul Jaber and striker Qahtan Chither were fingered as the main culprits and were whipped for three days by Uday's bodyguards.

When Iraq failed to reach the 1994 World Cup finals, Uday recalled the squad for extra training - with a concrete ball.

The Royal gaffer

The rarely-used title Royal Dictator was first applied in 1938 to King Carol II of Romania, one of the most controversial members of Queen Elizabeth II's extended royal family.

Carol enjoyed a sex life that was the subject of much fantastic and lurid speculation. The Queen's cousin, it was widely alleged, slept with thousands of women and created the post of full time court abortionist to keep pace with his impregnations (it was rumoured that the dictator-king was so abnormally well-endowed that sex proved fatal for several of his mistresses and that a slush fund was set up to silence their families).

Carol insisted on picking his country's soccer team for the 1930 World Cup Finals, where they beat Peru 3–1 and narrowly failed to reach the semi-finals by going out to the hosts and eventual winners Uruguay. History will remember King Carol as a dangerous, power-mad despot whose record in World Cup football was much better than those of England managers Graham Taylor, Kevin Keegan, Steve McClaren or Fabio Capello.

Puckish

Alexander Lukashenko's passions for ice hockey and rollerblading are subjects of national importance in the state of Belarus. Senior government officials are often seen rollerblading alongside him in public and whenever the president fancies a scratch game of ice hockey, inside closed arenas, his team mates - professionals, businessmen and personal bodyguards - have been known to leave their sickbeds to take part. The president wears a number 1 shirt and has his own bench where no one is allowed to talk to him. His team always wins.

In 2014 writers, artists and film directors from half a dozen countries called for a boycott of the first ever major international sporting event in Belarus, the world ice hockey championships, behind the campaign slogan "Lukashenko, Puck You'.

Old man river

Chairman Mao was a swimming fanatic. He liked to be seen swimming in the choppy waters off the north China coast, where the Party leadership met for its annual conferences, and took the plunge in the heavily polluted rivers of south China, despite the best advice of his guards and doctors, breast-stroking his through chunks of gently bobbing human ordure.

When rumours of Mao's declining health began to circulate in the 1970s, the Chinese Communist Party published clumsily doctored photographs showing their Chairman's disembodied head bobbing on the waves, purporting to show him swimming in the ocean. Mao's oceanic dips were always strictly for propaganda purposes: the Great Helmsman had heated swimming pools built in every one of his 55 homes.

Shooting practice

During a soccer match in Tripoli in 1997, a team sponsored by Libyan president Muammar Gaddafi's son was at the receiving end of a questionable refereeing decision and sparked a mass brawl between players. When fans jeered, Gaddafi's bodyguards opened fire on them. Some spectators returned fire, resulting in a death toll by some estimates as high as fifty. Gaddafi declared a period of mourning, during which time all TV broadcasts were transmitted in black and white only. The gesture went largely unnoticed, as no one in Libya owned a colour TV.

PROFILE: GENERAL NE WIN

Born: Shu Maung on 24 May 1911

Died: 5 December 2002

Also known as: The Old Man; The Puppet Master; Number One

Occupation: President of Burma 1962 - 1988

Hobbies: an obsession with the number nine; drinking, gambling and women, was said to bathe daily in dolphins' blood to regain his youthful vigour

Career highlight: told reporters at his one and only press conference, "Motherfuckers. Why do you want a press conference? What do you want me to say?"

Career lowlight: kicked out of university in 1931 after failing his biology exam, he was so annoyed that he decided to start a revolution; his first act in power was to massacre protesting students and to blow up the students' union building

Significant others: married five times, once to an Italian actress

Style: increasingly bizarre behaviour; imagined himself to be the reincarnation of an ancient Burmese warrior king and liked to dress up as one

Personality cult status:
his adopted name means 'Brilliant Like The Sun'. Said to be obsessed with his legacy, In his final years was increasingly absorbed in Buddhist scriptures and hoped to gain immortality by erecting a huge gold-domed pagoda in Rangoon.

Whimsical cruelty factor:
invented the 'helicopter ride', whereby victims were hung by their wrists or ankles from a rotating ceiling fan then beaten as it turned. Beat a colleague to death with a club on the golf course.

PROFILE: SAPARMURAT NIYAZOV

Born: 19 February 1940

Died: 20 December 2006

Also known as: Turkmenbashi (Father of all the Turks); the Moonlike Prophet

Occupation: First and Eternal President of Turkmenistan from 1991 - 2006

Hobbies: building monuments, poetry - he previewed his collection of prose *The Three Evils Threatening Our Homeland* ('indiscipline', 'arrogance' and 'wayward thinking' in case you were wondering) on live TV, moments after sacking the commander-in-chief of the armed forces. Previous literary works include the epic *White Wheat*, dedicated to Turkmenistan's harvest and *Mother*, dedicated to his late mother

Career highlights: (1) renaming the month of April and the word for 'bread' after his mother (2) he 'banned' a host of infectious diseases, including AIDS and cholera, by declaring them 'unlawful'

Career lowlight: his image adorned the nation's stamps and currency, causing a costly recall when his dyed black hair turned permanently white after a quadruple heart bypass operation in 2001

Significant others: his late mother Gurbansoltan, who he lost in an earthquake in 1948 when he was eight

Style: king of post-Soviet bling. Dyed hair, which alternated between jet black and punk red.

Personality cult status:
omnipresent even by the standards of cult dictatorship. Towns, mosques, factories, power plants, universities, airports, brands of aftershave, vodka, yogurt, tea and even a meteor are named in his honor. Among the hundreds of monuments to Turkmenbashi, the most conspicuous was a 120-foot golden statue in the capital, Ashgabat, erected on a motorised plinth. The monument rotates a full 360 degrees every twenty-four hours so that the president's arm always points to the sun, (although some say it was the other way around). Every town in Turkmenistan has a Turkmenbashi Street; confusingly, Ashgabat had several until he replaced all the street names in the capital with numbers. He was planning to build an ice castle in the middle of the desert when he died, appropriately, on Stalin's birthday

Whimsical cruelty factor:
a pioneer of psychological torture, forced his countrymen watch his private TV channel, which has no foreign news, only traditional singing and dancing and all-day readings of Niyazov's poems. Niyazov's book *Rukhnama* (Book of the Soul), a compilation of reinvented history, folklore and pseudo-philosophical maxims was required reading for students, married couples and applicants for a driver's license.

PROFILE: JUAN PERON

Born: 8 October 1895

Died: 1 July 1974

Also known as: El Lider

Occupation: President of Argentina 1946 - 55 and 1973 - 74

Hobbies: throwing house parties for notorious Nazi war criminals; his friend the 'Angel of Death' Dr. Josef Mengele lived so openly under Peron's protection that he was listed in the Buenes Aires phone book.

Career highlight: swept to power in 1946 after addressing a euphoric mass rally of 300,000 'shirtless ones'

Career lowlight: sharing a dinner table with the corpse of his deceased wife Eva

Significant others: wives Eva Duarte (Evita) and Isabel: while petitioning the Pope to have Eva beatified, had an affair with a 14-year-old girl.

Style: sharp suits and dazzling good looks caused ladies at Peronist rallies to flash their panties and beg to bear his children

Personality cult status:
although dead since 1974, he and Eva are still revered as icons by the Peronist Party

Whimsical cruelty factor:
combined Medieval-style crudity with twentieth century innovation; on a busy day his death squads employed genital mutilations, gang rapes, skin peeling, burning with hot coals and acids and immersion in human sewage. The repertoire included the 'telephone,' an electric prod attached to the mouth and ears, the 'helmet of death', an electrode studded device placed on the victim's head and electrode studded underwear and the picana, a 12,000 volt electrical device attached to nipples, the soles of the feet or sexual organs, causing unbearable pain (and sterility) without trace; the body of the victim was always doused with water first for better conductivity.

PROFILE: POL POT

Born: Solath Sar on 19 May 1925

Died: 15 April 1998

Also known as: Brother Number One

Occupation: Prime Minister of Cambodia 1975 - 79

Career highlight: after leading the Khmer Rouge guerrilla forces to victory in 1975, declared Year Zero, a radical attempt to create a communist utopia

Career lowlight: living in the jungle on the run from the police, plagued with gastric problems and suspecting he was being poisoned, survived by eating lizards

Significant others: first wife Khieu Ponnary (Sister Number One); she went mad in the late 1970's so he had her committed to a mental institution and took a much younger second wife, Mea Som.

Style: grey Mao suits or black pyjamas, the working attire of the Khmer Rouge

Personality cult status: none to speak of. Unlike every other totalitarian regime in the 20th century Pol Pot was publicity shy and his image was rarely seen

Whimsical cruelty factor:
executed people with stone axes to save on bullets. Infringements punishable by death included not working hard enough, complaining about living conditions, stealing food, wearing jewelry, engaging in sexual relations, grieving over the loss of relatives or friends, expressing religious sentiments, knowing a foreign language or wearing glasses

CHAPTER EIGHT
LEADERS AT LEISURE

Crème de la Kremlin

After sentencing thousands of innocent people to death with a stroke of the pen, Stalin liked nothing more than to settle down in his private cinema to enjoy a good American cowboy movie.

He kept a secret stash of American films, mostly Tarzans and westerns, for his private viewing pleasure, commanding the presence of a translator. The translator was so terrified of saying the wrong thing that he usually stuck to describing the visual action that Stalin could see for himself.

'Uncle Joe' also loved a good politically correct home grown musical. Among his favourite Soviet songfests were *Tractor Drivers*, *The Swineherd and the Shepherd* and *Hard Work, Happy Holiday*, featuring joyous harvest crews of dancing girls in overalls, singing lines such as 'the quota has been attained' and 'our love blossoms like the wheat'.

He saw his favourite Russian film *Volga, Volga* (1938) more than one hundred times and once offered a copy to President Franklin Roosevelt.

Stalin's favourite actress was Lyubov Orlova, wife of the film director Grigori Alexandrov. When he met Orlova at the film studios he was surprised by how thin she was. "Doesn't your husband feed you?" he asked, "... then we'll shoot him." He was joking, for once.

In 1934 Grigori Alexandrov's *The Jolly Fellows* was banned by Soviet film censors because it was 'ideologically unsound', but Stalin liked the film and had the ban lifted. "Anyone who made a movie as funny as this one" Stalin told Alexandrov, "has to be a brave man."

Stalin's film censor Ivan Boshakov, head of the Central Film Industry Directorate, lived with the knowledge that his two cinematic predecessors had been shot. Once asked by a filmmaker for an opinion of his work before Stalin had seen it, Bolshakov shrugged: "I don't know what I think of it yet."

Uncle Joe was very prudish. Once, when Bolshakov showed him a film with a nude dancer in it, he asked: "Are you running a brothel, Bolshakov?" and stormed out. In the original cut of Volga Volga Stalin was shocked by a passionate French kiss and had it removed. For a while, kissing was banned from all Soviet movies.

Although he enjoyed cowboy movies, especially the work of director John Ford, Stalin decided that Ford's star actor John Wayne, who was a vociferous anti-Communist, was a threat to the cause and should be assassinated. A hit squad was supposedly sent to Hollywood but failed to complete its' mission before Stalin's death.

When his successor Khrushchev met the actor in 1958 he apologised; "that was the decision of Stalin in his last mad years. I rescinded the order."

Der Fartenfûhrer

Medical historians agree that Hitler was the victim of uncontrollable flatulence. He tried to cure himself when he was a rising politician by poring over medical manuals, coming to the conclusion that a meatless diet would calm his turbulent digestion as well as make his farts less offensive: at one point he tried to cure himself by drinking machine gun oil.

Although he was vegetarian Adolf often lapsed; according to his cook, he was partial to sausages and stuffed pigeon. Adolf also examined his own faeces on a regular basis and gave himself camomile enemas.

Hitler was strangely oblivious by the fact that this high-fibre diet was having the opposite effect to which it was intended: His private physician Dr. Theo Morell noted in his diary after Hitler enjoyed a typical vegetable meal: "constipation and colossal flatulence occurred on a scale I have seldom encountered before." Adolf spent his final hours eating chocolate cake.

* * *

Hitler was considered the world's most boring dinner party host by most who kept company with him. He once entertained his guests by marching up and down the room imitating different sorts of artillery fire.

Big in Albania

The only Western films shown in Albania during Enver Hoxha's reign were those starring the English slapstick comic Norman Wisdom - or 'Pitkin', as his Albanian fans knew him.

No one is quite sure why Wisdom's films alone escaped censorship; it may have been that Hoxha considered them ideologically sound; the downtrodden Norman Pitkin's struggles against the decadent Mr. Grimsdale in such films as *Pitkini Ne Dyqan* (Pitkin At The Store) and *Pitkini Ne Spital* (Pitkin In The Hospital) were interpreted as a Communist parable on the class war, showing a member of the oppressed proletariat triumphing against capitalism.

Or it could have been that the plot lines were just so silly that even Hoxha's legendary paranoia was not alerted. In any event, as the country's only permitted Western film star, Norman Wisdom became Albania's second biggest national folk hero after Mother Teresa.

Pasta imperfect

Benito Mussolini was convinced that Italy's lack of fighting spirit was down to eating pasta. The Roman legions, *Il Duce* reasoned, had survived on a diet of stodgy barley porridge and conquered the known world, while his own soldiers struggled even to defeat Albania on a diet of spaghetti.

According to the fascist leader, flaccid tagliatelle was symbolic of the Italian male's lost virility.

End of the line

The reclusive Kim Jong-Il travelled little, and only ever in a train because of his fear of flying, a phobia he was believed to share with his father. His private train journeys were luxurious, despite the millions left behind starving due to famine: a Russian emissary who travelled across Russia with Kim described how live lobsters were airlifted daily to his train. He was on a train in Pyongyang when he died of a heart attack.

Mean cuisine

The former emperor of the Central African Republic, Jean Bedel-Bokassa, found himself in the dock in December, 1986, two months after returning from exile.

The highlights of his trial was when his former cook, Philippe Linguissa, recalled that whenever his employer needing cheering up, he would order a slice off the leader of the opposition, whose stuffed carcass was kept in Bokassa's extra-large deep-freeze. In his defence, Bokassa explained to the court: "I'm not a saint. I'm just a man like everyone else."

Adolf's sibling

Adolf Hitler had a half-brother, Alois, and a sister-in-law, Bridget, who lived in Liverpool, England. Bridget Hitler tried to cash in on her family connection by writing a book, *My Brother-in-Law Adolf*, but couldn't find a publisher. The most surprising and unprovable claim in the 225-page typescript was that Adolf spent six months with them at their flat at 102 Upper Stanhope Street, Liverpool from November 1912. Hitler never once mentioned his visit to England, according to Bridget, because he was avoiding compulsory service in the Austrian army.

The supposed trip however may have had a lasting impression on *der Führer*. Before adopting his famous toothbrush moustache, he experimented with a variety of facial hairstyles from a 'full set' to a pointed goatee; according to his sister, at the time of his trip to England he was sporting a large handlebar moustache. Before he took leave of his sister-in-law in May 1913 Bridget advised him to trim it. Years later when she saw his picture in a newspaper she saw that he had taken her advice, but noted in her book: 'Adolf had gone too far.'

Jailbait

As a communist guerrilla fighter, Enver Hoxha was forced to eat boiled gravel for three years. He made up for it when he became president of Albania; to ensure the conservation of supplies of his favourite dish, Hoxha made it illegal to fish for red-speckled trout; the penalty for catching one was fifteen years' hard labour.

Dragon breath

Chairman Mao acquired an epic personal hygiene problem that grew steadily worse with old age. For over a quarter of a century never once took a bath, although he did allow his servants to wipe him down every so often with a wet towel. During the Chinese civil war in 1947 his doctor reproached him for using the same towel to dry both his face and feet. Mao refused to buy another one, saying: "if every soldier refrains from buying a second towel, we shall be able to stage a second great campaign."

Mao scorned toothbrushes on the basis that "tigers never brush their teeth", preferring to rinse his mouth out with tea once every morning. His teeth became covered with a heavy green film before they eventually turned black and fell out. In his later years he lived almost exclusively on stewed bamboo and stir-fried lettuce. Mao never ate fish for dinner: he routinely took strong sleeping pills before his evening meal and would often fall asleep mid-chew. His aides were expected to remove the food from his mouth: fish bones could have been fatal.

Il Duce's diet

Mussolini secretly suffered from a variety of health problems including a crippling gastric ulcer that caused him to roll on the carpet in agony. He lived mostly on milk, drinking up to three litres a day to subdue his dreadful stomach-ache. When he met Hitler he was careful to eat alone so as to keep his strange diet a secret because he thought it was a bit 'unfascist'.

Mussolini was very careful to portray himself as a man of virile, robust health. He shaved his head so no one could see that his hair was turning grey and although his eyesight was poor, was never seen wearing spectacles in public. Although his doctors were generally reticent in their public pronouncements, Dr. Aldo Castellani, an expert in tropical diseases, revealed that Mussolini in fact suffered from intestinal worms. According to Castellani, the roundworm which eventually emerged from an unspecified orifice of *Il Duce* was enormous, "a real hypertrophic fascist ascaris".

One hump or two?

The Libyan leader Colonel Muammar Gaddafi regularly flew planeloads of camels to international conferences then parked them on the hotel lawns. It was the only way he could guarantee a supply of fresh camel milk.

In 2007 when the British Prime Minister Tony Blair visited Tripoli, he was advised by the foreign office; "if you are offered camel's milk in your tea, refuse as it causes uncontrollable farting".

Holy cow

The favourite dish of North Korea's Dear Leader Kim Jong-Il was roast donkey eaten with silver chopsticks. In North Korea this delicacy is known as 'heavenly cow', out of respect to Kim Jong-Il's late father, Kim Il-sung, who was not partial to donkey.

A dictator's best friend

After a hard day at the office Adolf Hitler would go home and give his German shepherd dog Blondi and his blonde mistress Eva a little pat on the head. Of the two, it was said, Hitler liked the dog more, because unlike Eva it didn't smoke.

When Adolf committed suicide he tested a lethal dose of cyanide on Blondi by crushing a capsule between her teeth. According to witnesses, the death of his dog caused him more distress than proposing the suicide of his recent bride, whom he married 36 hours earlier.

* * *

Both Hitler and his Axis partner Mussolini were aliurophobic - they suffered from an aversion to cats.

Tyrant tunes

Stalin banned jazz. Hitler banned Mendelssohn because he was Jewish but revered Richard Wagner as an artistic god.

* * *

Enver Hoxha banned the teaching of all music composed after 5 March 1953 - the date of Stalin's death.

* * *

Chairman Mao banned *The Sound Of Music* because it was "a blatant example of capitalist pornography."

* * *

The Malawian dictator Hastings Banda banned the song *Delilah* made famous by Tom Jones, in deference to a favourite mistress of the same name.

* * *

Mahmoud Ahmadinejad President of Iran, is a fan of the Irish crooner Chris de Burgh; his favourite record is de Burgh's *Lady In Red.* In 2009 de Burgh became the first Western artist given permission to perform gig in Iran since the Islamic revolution 30 years earlier, but his shows were cancelled following Ahmadinejad's crackdown on post-election protests.

* * *

The African despot Robert Mugabe had a touching devotion to British institutions, including Sir Cliff Richard. When told that Bob Marley would be performing at Zimbabwe's 1980 Independence Day celebrations, Mugabe complained that the reggae icon was too scruffy, suggesting Sir Cliff instead. Sadly, the perennially wholesome singer was otherwise engaged, so Marley sang at Mugabe's tear gas-stained concert in front of 100,000 people, including special guests Indira Gandhi and Prince Charles.

* * *

Kim Jong-Il may have prohibited "uproarious western music" in favour of "lively and militant marches", but was secretly a bit of a rocker. He once invited the Brit bluesman Eric Clapton to perform in North Korea, but Slowhand declined.

In Stalin's shoes

Chairman Mao hated wearing new shoes (he always had his bodyguards wear them in first) but his Marxist mentor Stalin had something of a boot fetish.

The son of a cobbler, Stalin worked as an apprentice in a Tbilisi shoe factory before he rose to become Russia's greatest tyrant and never forgot his humble origins; cobblers, whenever he encountered them, were surprised to find themselves engaged with their leader in animated conversations about footwear.

In 1918 a shoemaker in Tsaritsyn received a rare and dangerous commission; he was required to make a pair of high, black riding boots to Stalin's exact specification.

From that day he go them Stalin was rarely seen without boots, even on the most inappropriate and uncomfortable situations. In middle age, when he was plagued by corns, he stuck to his trusty old boots and cut holes in them to relieve the pain.

His footwear struck colleagues and visitors alike, sometimes literally. A guest once asked Stalin why he never took his boots off even on a stiflingly hot day. The Soviet leader replied, "So I can kick someone in the head with them so hard he'll never find all his teeth."

* * *

Although not quite in the same league as Imelda Marcos, Saddam Hussein also had a passion for expensive footwear, the indulgence of a man who had gone barefoot as a peasant boy. He had three guards killed because they tried to steal some of his shoes. He and George W. Bush owned three identical pairs of black leather crocodile leather shoes made by the Italian designer Vito Antioli.

Strange bedfellows

Hitler's cohorts were subject to intense Allied propaganda about their private lives, orchestrated by a secret department deep within the British foreign office. The supposed sexual peccadilloes of the most senior Nazis were contained in files marked 'Retain or Destroy' and headed 'Adults Only.'

The files alleged that Hitler's SS chief Heinrich Himmler was head of a cult that routinely indulged in group sex, egged on by the encouraging chanting of the high priestess Ursula Deinert of the Berlin state opera. Other propaganda leaflets told of wife swapping parties in Munich, where naked girls on white horses sang Ride of the Valkyries. There was even a Nazi update on 'spin the bottle'; a naked girl was strapped to a roulette wheel with Nazi leader Christian Weber acting as croupier.

Inevitably, Hitler's sex life was the subject of the thickest foreign office file of all, most of it contradictory. There were many rumours that he was homosexual, encouraged by his political enemies within the Third Reich. Several of his closest Nazi Party confidantes were gay, including his Deputy Rudolf Hess, known to some as 'Hitler's First Lady', and on whom the Soviet KGB kept a dossier, including details of his habit of painting his toenails red, filed under his supposed name in homosexual circles, 'Black Paula'.

Hitler's failure to rise above the rank of lance corporal, in spite of his heroism in World War I, which had earned him two Iron Crosses, was rumoured to be the penalty for a court-martial on a charge of indecency with a senior officer. Another senior Nazi official alleged that Hitler's military record contained two convictions for pederasty. In any event, after Hitler came to power the Gestapo destroyed the details of his military record. German womanhood by and large found Hitler highly fanciable; his penetrating eyes and ranting speeches, it was said, drove female listeners at his rallies to orgasm. Even allowing for the taint of Allied disinformation, *der Führer's* sex life was undeniably odd. He enjoyed a couple of affairs with actresses, including the young German film star Renate Muller. She claimed that above all Hitler enjoyed lying on the floor while being savagely kicked.

He enjoyed a 'special' relationship with his niece Angelika 'Geli' Raubal, nineteen years his junior and the daughter of his half-sister Angela. Geli confided to a friend that 'Uncle Alf' liked her to squat over his face and defecate on his head. She was found dead in Hitler's apartment, officially a suicide, eight months before he became Chancellor.

Adolf devoted thirteen pages to syphilis in *Mein Kampf,* describing it as a 'Jewish disease' that was 'transmitted generationally and destroyed races, nations, and ultimately mankind'.

Hitler however displayed many of the symptoms of advanced

syphilis, including encephalitis (inflammation of the brain), dizziness, neck pustules and chest pains. According to some sources he caught syphilis from a Jewish prostitute in Vienna around 1908; according to other accounts, he was given the diagnosis at a German field hospital in 1918 when he was recovering from a gas attack. Heinrich Himmler, the SS chief, saw to it that his army medical records were all destroyed.

Eva Braun, who spent her last ten years with Hitler, was said to have confided to friends that their relationship was completely sexless. Her diary entries on the subject of their sex life were obscure: in one she noted obliquely, 'he needs me for special reasons'.

Fellow Nazi Ernst 'Putzi' Habfstaengl, a personal friend of Hitler's in the early years, believed that *der Führer* was repressed and doubted that he ever experienced orthodox sexual relations with any woman. A leading British spy concurred, describing Eva Braun's relations with Hitler as 'of a platonic nature'. Testimonies of der Führer's lovers all agreed on one thing – his repellent body odor, the result of chronic flatulence. Lina Basquette, who had an affair with Adolf, regretted later; "Maybe if I hadn't been so fastidious I could have changed history, but, oh, that body odour of his!"

Pulp fiction

Hitler's favourite author was Karl May, a German writer of cheap American-style westerns. During the war he admonished his generals for their 'lack of imagination' and recommended they all read Karl May.

Hitler needed reading glasses but was too vain to wear them. At his insistence, all of his memoranda were printed out in banner headlines, requiring the invention of a special 'Führer typewriter' equipped with very large keys.

Power dressing

Mao Zedong's regulation grey military-style 'Mao suit' was

the ultimate fashion statement of proletarian unity. When it made its first appearance in 1949 the style wasn't an immediate hit with Mao's communist party apparatchiks: his chief of protocol Yu Yinqing suggested in future he stick to the more conventional dark suit when he was receiving foreign dignitaries. Yu's fashion tip went unheeded; he was fired and later committed suicide.

Fashion for fascists

Benito Mussolini had a famously eccentric dress sense. When the king of Italy summoned him to form a government, *Il Duce* arrived wearing a black shirt, jodhpurs, spats and a bowler hat. Realizing that his attire was probably slightly over the top for an audience with royalty, Mussolini excused himself by explaining, "I have just come from the front." In fact he had just come from his office. He stopped wearing bowler hats in 1930 when he found out that people were likening him to the comedian Oliver Hardy.

Of mice and maniacs

Hitler was delighted with his Christmas present from the Nazi Party's second greatest monster, Josef Goebbels in 1937 - fifteen Mickey Mouse cartoon films. Four years later however The Nazis declared Mickey an enemy of the Third Reich and banned him in Germany, Hitler's propagandist insisting that "mice are dirty".
At US Government behest, Walt Disney countered with anti-Hitler films and cartoons caricaturing Hitler. The mouse had the last word. After the war Mickey returned to West Germany and firmly established his reputation as a comic hero.

Sexual healing

Chinese Communist Party workers found that the best way to keep their leader Chairman Mao happy was with a permanent supply of nubile young females from politically correct peasant stock. Mao believed he could achieve longevity by increasing his number of sexual partners: at the height of the Cultural Revolution he was often to be found naked wrestling in enormous feather beds with three, four or even five young female volunteers simultaneously.

Mao's sexual appetite, if not always his performance, increased with age. Well into his seventies he was still shedding his drab military uniform to bed several young women at a time. Temporary bouts of impotence were variously treated by doctors with injections of ground deer antlers and a secret formula called H3. Mao frequently suffered from venereal disease but refused any treatment or to abstain from sex until the infection cleared. The young girls he regularly slept with though that catching VD from their Chairman was a badge of honour and proof of their close personal relationships to Mao. According to his physician Dr. Li, Mao had an undescended testicle, but because of his general ignorance of human physiology didn't realise that it wasn't normal. No one ever dared tell him otherwise.

Pox Romana

Mussolini's sex life was a key part of his appeal and went some way towards explaining his mass popularity. Although married with five children, he had a string of mistresses and illegitimate offspring. He liked his women plump and had sex with them where he could, on the edge of his office desk or up against a wall and always with his boots on.

Mussolini claimed he received a grenade wound in the First World War - a lie to conceal a dose of syphilis caught in 1907 from an older married woman. He was so relieved to receive a doctor's report stating that he was finally clear of infection after fifteen years of treatment that he thought about sharing his good news by making the report public, but his political advisers talked him out of it.

Gaddafi's five a day

The Libyan leader Colonel Muammar 'Mad Dog' Gaddafi was routinely described in the Western press as 'eccentric'. In his autobiography *Fighting for Peace*, former US Defence Secretary Casper Weinberger noted: "rumours had long circulated in intelligence circles that Gaddafi suffered from an incurable venereal disease and that this accounted for his occasional bouts of madness, in which hysteria, braggadocio and extreme theatricalism were all mixed."

The CIA was in no doubt, claiming that Gaddafi was impotent, insane and a cross-dresser. How did they know? According to a CIA report filed in 1985, Gaddafi was seen making a trip to Majorca wearing make-up and carrying a teddy bear.

Gaddafi's chef and manservant, Faisal, was entrusted to apply Gaddafi's make-up and dye his hair. His position also ensured he witnessed the despot's sexual excesses, driven by extensive use of Viagra, which ran to up to five women a day. The head of Gaddafi's private office was once sent to Pigalle, the sex district of Paris, to buy a machine that was supposed to lengthen Gaddafi's penis.

Dictator Dons

The Godfather was not only Saddam Hussein's favourite film, it was also a big influence on his management style. Saddam had at least fifty-three of his relatives killed, including two sons-in-law, the Kamel brothers.

In August 1995, following a fallout with Saddam's son Uday, the brothers defected to Jordan taking their wives with them. After telling the CIA everything they knew about Iraq's weapons programme the brothers became homesick and wanted to go home. Their father-in-law promised that no harm would come to them if they did. Borrowing a line almost directly from the mouth of Michael Corleone, Saddam asked Hussein Kamel, "Would I kill the father of my grandchildren?"

He had them shot immediately upon their return.

Coincidentally *The Godfather* was also the favourite film of North Korean dictator Kim Jong-Il. Kim owned more than 20,000 videos, although his taste in films was less than revolutionary, judging by his extensive library of western classics, especially John Wayne films, or his comprehensive collection of Daffy Duck cartoons and full set of James Bond films.

When he saw *Die Another Day*, in which he was parodied as the insane, power-mad son of a North Korean dictator, he was so annoyed that he stabbed his Minister of Culture with a ballpoint pen and spat at the screen.

Night music

Stalin lived a nocturnal existence and had a habit of phoning people in the middle of the night. Once he called the head of the State Broadcasting House to enquire about a Mozart piano concerto he had heard on the radio; "who was the pianist and could he get a recording of it?" enquired the man of steel. The radio chief broke into a cold sweat; no such recording existed, but he was too afraid to tell Stalin.

There was no alternative but to summon all the members of the orchestra and the pianist to the recording studio in the middle of the night and make a recording of the concerto, to be delivered to Stalin in the morning. This record was still on the turntable when Stalin died.

Nazi habit

Stalin and Chairman Mao were both cigarette chain-smokers. When Mao's doctor advised him to cut down on his lifelong three-pack-a-day habit he countered; "smoking is also a form of deep-breathing exercise, don't you think?"

* * *

Hitler was a heavy smoker in his early life, but quit and became fanatical member of the ant-smoking lobby. According to *der Führer,* tobacco was "the wrath of the red man against the white man, vengeance for having been given hard liquor". Adolf attributed his personal success to non-smoking, claiming in 1942; "I am convinced that if I had been a smoker, I never would have been able to bear the cares and anxieties which have been a burden to me for so long. Perhaps the German people owe their salvation to that fact."

He also banned smoking in his bunker and gave gold watches to associates who kicked the habit; it didn't stop them lighting up the moment they heard he had committed suicide.

* * *

When president Niyazov quit smoking in 1997 after undergoing heart surgery, the entire population of Turkmenistan was obliged to follow suit.

Autocrats

Although Adolf Hitler never learned to drive he was the driving force behind the development of Professor Porsche's KdF-wagen - the 'Strength Through Joy' car, or Volkswagen Beetle as it came to be known. He sketched the original Beetle design on a napkin at a restaurant table in Munich in 1932. Adolf preferred to be driven along his new *autobahn* in big, powerful, bombproof Mercedes-Benz. His preference was for eight-cylinder open-topped models, such as the six-wheeled Mercedes G-4.

Hitler was so proud of his country's automobile industry that in 1939, when Nazi Germany and the Soviet Union signed their pact of non-aggression, he gave a supercharged sports Mercedes roadster to his good friend, Joe Stalin.

Adolf had a mutual admirer in Henry Ford, the only American mentioned in *Mein Kampf.* Hitler kept a framed photograph of Ford on his desk; Ford returned the favour and kept a photo of Hitler on his desk in Dearborn, Michigan.

Adolf awarded Ford the V*erdienstkreutz Deutscher Adler* (the Grand Service Cross of the Supreme Order of the German

Eagle) in 1938 on the American's seventy-eighth birthday in recognition of his pioneering work in the auto industry and in making the car available to the masses. Ford was very happy to receive it.

* * *

The Soviet Union's homegrown ZIS - Zavod Imiena Stalina – was originally named after Stalin, but later renamed ZIL. Stalin's personal favourite, a special 1949 ZIS eight-cylinder limousine, was a 20 foot long, 7 ton behemoth with 3 inch thick bulletproof glass. It did about 4mph on a good run.

Stalin once presented Chairman Mao with five ZIS bulletproof stretch limousines with art deco style red flags on their crest. Mao was so impressed that he commissioned a homemade, 10-metre long, luxury six-door stretch 'Red Flag' limousine, complete with fridge, telephone, TV, double bed, desk and sofa. He died in 1976 before he could use what would become the first, and last, limo produced by China's First Automobile Works.

* * *

Hitler is often credited for inventing the motorway, but that honour goes to Benito Mussolini, who ordered the construction of the first *autostrada* toll way between Milan and the northern Italian lakes, completed in 1923. Germany's first *autobahn* was built between Cologne and Bonn in 1929, before Hitler came to power.

* * *

Vladimir Ilyich Lenin, the father of the Russian revolution, liked to travel in style and owned nine Rolls-Royces. One, a Silver Ghost open tourer, is exhibited in the Lenin museum of Moscow. His was not the first Rolls-Royce in Russia; Czar Nicholas II had two Silver Ghosts and Josef Stalin also had a Roller, as did Leonid Brezhnev; part of his extensive car collection.

* * *

'Papa Doc' Duvalier travelled in a Mercedes 600, throwing wads of banknotes out of the window as he went. The Mercedes stretch limo is so popular among African despots (President Mobutu of Zaire owned fifty-one of them) that the political elite is known in Swahili as wabenzi - 'men of Mercedes-Benz'.

* * *

The North Korean leader Kim Il-sung had every road in the country built with an extra lane for his sole private use.

Ne win situation

In 1970 the Burmese dictator General Ne Win announced that it had been revealed to him in a dream that all of his countrymen should stop driving on the left-hand side of the road and switch to the right. As most of the cars in Rangoon were old British right-hand-drive models, Burma quickly became the world leader in road fatalities.

PROFILE: JOSEPH STALIN

Born: Josef Vissarionovich Dzhugashvili on 21 December 1879

Died: 5 March 1953

Also known as: Uncle Joe

Occupation: Premier of the Soviet Union 1941 - 53

Hobbies: gardening, poetry, playing billiards and watching US movies: he saw his favourite, the 1938 film *Boys Town* starring Spencer Tracy at least 25 times

Career highlight: in a single day in December 1938, 'Uncle Joe' signed 3,182 death warrants

Career lowlight: left to die in a puddle of urine on the floor by attendants, who were too afraid to enter his bedroom uninvited

Significant others: wives Ekaterina and Nadezhda: the latter committed suicide.

Style: big boots, big moustaches, super heroic statuary, extreme paranoia

Personality cult status:
the first dictator to employ a highly sophisticated propaganda machine. In the arts and in everyday life the physical image of Stalin was ever-present.

Whimsical cruelty factor:
had prisoners beaten so hard that their eyeballs literally popped out; deaths during interrogation were always registered as heart attacks.

PROFILE: ALFREDO STROESSNER

Born: 3 November 1912

Also known as: the Luminous Lighthouse, Colonel Trunk

Occupation: President of Paraguay 1954 - 89 (full title Generalissimo Alfredo Stroessner, Legion d'Honneur, Knight of the Order of St Michael and St George, Order of the Condor of the Andes, Medal of the Inter-American Junta of Defense, Collar of the Order of the Liberator and Grand Cross of the Order of the Sun with Diamonds)

Hobbies: hunting, fishing and sheltering retired dictators (Pinochet, Somoza) and an estimated 300 Nazi war criminals

Career highlight: meeting Prince Philip, Duke of Edinburgh during his tour of South America. The Queen's husband told him; "it's a pleasant change to be in a country that isn't ruled by its people"

Career lowlights: (1) in 1948 he found himself on the wrong side of a failed coup attempt and had to escape to the Brazilian embassy hidden in the boot of a car, an experience which earned him the nickname Colonel Trunk (2) in his seventies, while visiting one of several teenage mistresses for his regular Thursday afternoon siesta, heard that he had been ousted by his protégé and second-in-command, General Andres Rodriguez

Style: military chic - enough gold braid to hang an opposition party

Significant others: wife Dona and various teenage mistresses; sons Gustavo and Freddie Junior plus numerous illegitimate children.

Personality cult status:
relatively low key - i.e. just an airport and a city named after him and his photo displayed in every shop and workplace

Whimsical cruelty factor:
his imaginative torturer-in-chief Pastor Coronel conducted interrogations with interviewees while they were immersed in the *pileta* - a bathtub full of human excrement.

PROFILE: RAFAEL TRUJILLO

Born: Rafael Leonidas Trujillo Molina on 24 October 1891

Died: 30 May 1961

Also known as: Generalissimo; El Benefactor; El Jefe (the Chief), El Chibo (the Goat).

Occupation: President of the Dominican Republic 1930 - 61

Hobbies: tested the loyalty of his functionaries by sleeping with their wives and daughters - then obliging them to join in

Career highlight: winning the 1937 Dominican Baseball League Championship with his own team, the Cuidad Trujillo Dragons

Career lowlight: incontinent and approaching his seventieth birthday, he was cut down in a hail of machine gun fire on his way to visit his twenty year old mistress

Significant others: three wives, Aminta, Bienvenida and Maria and four 'favorite' mistresses, Lina, Elsa, Norma and Mony

Style: Sergeant Pepper uniforms and dark glasses

Personality cult status: according to the *Guinness Book of Records* ran the world's most omnipresent dictatorship. Literally put himself on an equal footing with God. Spent millions building monuments to himself all over the country and renamed the country's capital Trujillo City.

Whimsical cruelty factor:
Fed his enemies to the sharks: had his doctor killed after he diagnosed the Generalissimo with prostate cancer.

CHAPTER NINE
DEAD DICTATORS

One dead S.O.B

The hard-line anti-communist Rafael Trujillo was a convicted rapist, a minor detail overlooked by the Dominican dictator's many friends in the US government. As Secretary of State Cordell Hull put it, "He may be a son of a bitch, but he is our son of a bitch."[2]

In 1961 relations between Trujillo and the White House became strained when the despot clumsily tried to retire his neighbour, the Venezuelan president Romulo Betancourt, with a large bomb. Embarrassingly for Trujillo, the attempt on Betancourt's life was publicly announced on Dominican radio half an hour before it actually took place. The Eisenhower administration did a swift U-turn and approved a CIA plan to remove their old ally.

On 30 May 1961, as Trujillo and his chauffeur were driving unescorted along a quiet country road, they were ambushed by two carloads of armed gunmen. The sixty-nine year old dictator stepped out of his car and tried to bluff his way out of impending death, but was shot twenty-nine times at point blank range, his body run over, tossed into the boot of another car, then dumped by the roadside on Santa Domingo's

---

[2] A sentiment Hull also expressed about the Nicaraguan dictator Anastasio Somoza.

George Washington Avenue.

Sadly, Trujillo's death, did not herald a new dawn of liberalism and human rights. His son Ramfis seized power and went after his father's killers with a vengeance. All but two of the conspirators died violently at the hands of the Trujillo family. One was fed the flesh of his own son, and then presented with his son's head on a plate; the father had a fatal heart attack. Another four were put to death by firing squad, their remains allegedly thrown to the sharks after their executions.

El Difunto

Paraguay's paranoid Perpetual Dictator Jose Francia, known informally as *El Supremo*, didn't allow anyone in his presence to stand within six paces of him and only then with their hands well away from their sides. At the age of seventy-nine Francia took to his bed with a chill. A physician was called to examine him, but when he strayed within the permitted distance, Francia stabbed him with a sabre. Untended, the dictator died the following day.

For several days, no-one dared believe that their leader was actually dead, sensing a trap. For decades after his death, Paraguayans were even afraid to mention his name: they referred to him only as *El Difunto* – the deceased.

Shrine on

When Lenin died in 1924 the Russians wanted to house their deceased leader in a mausoleum that surpassed anything else in the world in grandeur and magnificence.

Eventually they opted for a cube-shaped design which was supposed to represent a 'fourth dimension' where death did not exist. The designer, Shchusev, believed in the occult properties of cubes and suggested that Lenin's followers keep a small cube in their homes. His idea was adopted by the party and cubic shrines to the dead leader were set up in 'Lenin corners' in offices and factories.

Since his death in 1924 Lenin has managed to get through several dozen new suits. Under his blue acrylic tailored three-piece, the father of communism also wears a rubber wetsuit into which is poured the solution that keeps him from falling apart. Twice a week his hands and face are painted with fresh embalming fluid and every eighteen months the whole body is lifted out and given a thoroughly good soaking.

Every four years a bit of Lenin is scraped off, placed under a microscope and examined for signs of deterioration. At least 60 per cent of his body is now made of wax, including his ears. He is also said to have a growth of fungus around his neck and the back of his head that wasn't there when he led the Bolsheviks to power in 1917.

Lenin continues to be a crowd-puller in his mausoleum, although neither his reputation nor the queues are quite what they were.

Kim's necrocracy

When death came to Kim Il-sung at the age of 82 in July 1994, after a 100-day period of mourning the deceased dictator was promoted to Eternal Leader - forever the official head of state. The 'immortal and imperishable' late Kim Il-sung is currently resting in a glass coffin in a giant mausoleum, the Kumsusan Memorial Palace, where his skin is tweaked and powdered by Russian embalming experts once a month.

His speeches however remain as fresh as the day they were written. In 2007 the Publishing House of the Worker's Party of North Korea posthumously published the Complete Collection of Kim Il Sung's Works Volume 69, covering the period from January to August 1979, including some of Kim's greatest hits including the memorable *It Is Necessary To Intensify The Study of Methods of Cultivating Crops to Suit the Conditions of Alpine Areas.*

Fascist gonads

Adolf Hitler's charred remains were positively identified by his teeth, discovered by Soviet soldiers in a shallow grave outside his Berlin bunker in 1945 and since locked away in an archive in Moscow.

The post-mortem performed by Russian doctors on his partly burned body confirmed that, in the words of the old music hall song, *der Führer* did indeed have only one ball.

Medical historians were divided as to whether the missing gonad had been removed surgically, possibly as a result of a bullet in the groin during World War 1, or as was common practice when advanced syphilis reaches the fatal stage.

In 2008 an account left by the medic who treated Hitler during the Battle of the Somme in 1916 settled the matter by confirming that the famous testicle went missing on the Western Front. Dr. Johan Jambor told his priest that Hitler had been shot in the abdomen; apparently Adolf screamed a lot then asked him: "will I still be able to have children?"

There is however another version of events from the person who was best placed to know the truth. According to Eva Braun, Hitler's testicular damage was the result of a boyhood mishap with a wild alpine goat.

Hitler' ally the Spanish dictator General Franco also lost some of his manhood through injury sustained in battle. He was shot in the lower abdomen at El Biutz, near Ceuta, Morocco in June 1916 when was a captain in the Spanish army. He went on to father a daughter, Carmen Franco y Polo, in 1926. Ten years later he joined the military uprising that led to the Spanish Civil War and assumed leadership of the fascist party ruling Spain for 36 years with an iron fist, but only one ball.

Although he was one of the 20th century's most durable dictators, unlike his fascist contemporaries Hitler and Mussolini, Franco was not the most charismatic of leaders. Hitler once described meeting him as 'less pleasurable than having four or five teeth pulled'.

Severe illness forced Franco to resign in 1973, but he lingered on much longer than even his doctors or his supporters anticipated. On his deathbed at last two years later, Franco was told that General Garcia had arrived and wished to say goodbye. 'Why?' Franco enquired. 'Is Garcia going somewhere?'

Patient Number One

Seventy-four year old Stalin was about to launch his biggest leadership purge yet when he was felled by a fatal stroke and lay helpless on the floor in a pool of his own urine, unable to call for help.

As no one dared to go into his rooms uninvited it was hours before his bodyguards finally summoned up the courage to open his door, plenty of time for Stalin to reflect upon the fact that he had recently ordered the arrest and torture of most of his best doctors.

Eventually a maid sent for Stalin's highest ranking subordinate Lavrenti Beria, who took the curious decision to shut the door and leave his leader 'undiscovered' until the following morning - enough time for Beria to search through Stalin's safe and files for incriminating documents, including evidence against himself.

When help finally arrived, the terrified medics were reluctant even to touch Stalin to take his pulse, but leeches were applied to his ears and he was administered enemas of magnesium sulphate and spoonfuls of weak tea. 'Patient Number One', as he was referred to in his autopsy report, died five days later.

A few months later, Stalin's former right hand man was dramatically arrested and tried on thirty-nine counts of sexual assault; a search of Beria's office had revealed a large stash of female underwear. As neither his responsibility for mass murder in the Stalin era nor his own record as a multiple rapist could be publicly mentioned for fear of bringing the Communist regime into disrepute, Beria was declared guilty of a plot 'to revive capitalism' and summarily executed, his name wiped from public memory.

In true Stalinist tradition, subscribers to the *Great Soviet Encyclopedia* were helpfully advised to use 'a small knife or razor blade' to remove the entry on Beria and then to insert a replacement article on the Bering Sea.

Enver's disco

The Albanian dictator Enver Hoxha spent his last few years as a total recluse, dictating dense, rambling books lambasting his communist allies for betraying the Marxist cause.

His final book, *The Dangers of Anglo-Americans in Albania* warned his countrymen to watch out for hairy visitors, especially men with beards - cunning devices used to disguise British and American spies.

Hoxha suffered from a heart attack and died in the early hours of 11 April 1985. He had instructed his wife Nexhmije to build a pyramid after his death to house everything he owned. The huge, white, marble and glass Enver Hoxha Memorial Museum was duly stocked with the collected artifacts of the late dictator, including such vital state treasures as some of his old toiletries. After the fall of communism in Albania it became a disco.

Adolf's manhood?

In 2007 an enterprising Russian put up for sale what he claimed was Hitler's mummified penis for £12,00.

According to Ivan Zudropov, his ex-Red Army soldier father hacked it off as a souvenir after storming Adolf's command bunker in 1945: allegedly, the troops stripped Hitler's body of clothing then kicked and punched it before cutting it into pieces for souvenirs.

Zudropov said his father had wanted to steal Hitler's head, but thought better of it.

Red terror

Josef Stalin's successor, the Soviet leader Nikita Khrushchev, was scathing in his attacks on the late Soviet tyrant and his legacy. In a typical speech he once said:"There are still some people who think that we have Stalin to thank for all our progress, who quake before Stalin's dirty underpants, who stand at attention and salute them."

Khruschev was denouncing Stalin at a public meeting in similar fashion one day when he was heckled by his audience: "You were one of Stalin's colleagues" protested a voice from the crowd. "Why didn't you do something about it?" "Who said that?" Khrushchev demanded. The room fell completely silent. Khruschev continued quietly, "now you know why."

Animal magic

After a decade of bizarre and brutal dictatorship, in 1979 Macias Nguema, president of Equatorial Guinea, was overthrown in by his nephew Teodor and sentenced to death with six aides at the end of a four-day trial for murder, treason, embezzlement and genocide.

That evening, the seven were shot at Malabo's Blabich Prison. The firing squad was imported from Morocco because local troops refused to shoot their former boss; Nguema's spirit was too strong for mere bullets, they said, and he would undoubtedly return as a tiger.

Flesh in the pan

In 2009 the US rapper Eve reportedly dumped her boyfriend Teodori Obiang, the son of Equatorial Guinean dictator Teodoro Obiang Nguema Mbasogo, after a brief affair, upon learning that his dictator father was a cannibal.

Obiang wooed the star by lavishing her with luxury gifts, but 27-year-old Eve ended it when Severo Moto Nsa, the leader of the government in exile, noted; "He (Mbasogo) has just devoured a police commissioner. I say devoured, as this commissioner was buried without his testicles and brain."

The waxwork Helmsman

Although Chairman Mao had requested cremation, when he finally succumbed to a fatal neurological disorder in 1976 his designated successor Hua Guofeng overruled him; the late Chinese leader was to be preserved for all time.

Given the primitive state of Chinese embalming technology, it was a nigh impossible task. The decision had also been made too late, because Mao's vital organs should have been removed and the arteries and veins flushed out within two hours of death. To complicate matters further, the task of mummification fell to Mao's personal physician, Dr. Li Zhisui, who had never embalmed a corpse before.

To keep it in reasonable shape until the memorial service, Li pumped about 40 litres of formaldehyde into Mao's body - almost twice the advised limit. Mao's head was so full of embalming fluid that it made his ears stick out at right angles. Even so, this still didn't prevent his nose from falling off four weeks later.

Mao is now apparently shrinking at a steady rate of about five per cent a year. The official line given by the mausoleum director is that this is merely an optical illusion caused by the curious lighting effects in the hall which contains his corpse. Rumour has it however that Mao has long since been replaced by a wax dummy.

Esprit de corpse

In April 1945 Benito Mussolini tried to flee from the advancing Allied army but was found hiding in the back of a truck heading for the Alps. He tried to disguise himself by wearing a private's overcoat, but had forgotten to remove his striped general's pants.

He and his long-standing mistress Clara Petacci were executed on the spot by machine gun fire, then taken to the Piazzale Loreto in Milan where they were strung up by their feet with piano wire and left dangling from the girders of a petrol station. To protect her modesty, Petacci's skirt was discreetly tied about her legs with the belt of a chivalrous partisan, as a crowd gathered to spit at, kick and even pump more bullets into the exposed corpses.

Mussolini had already nominated an epitaph for his tomb: "Here lies one of the most intelligent animals who ever appeared on the face of the earth".

A year after his death his corpse was stolen from a supposedly secret, unmarked grave in a municipal cemetery by fascists intent on a publicity stunt. The remains were a symbol of the old order for those nostalgic for his regime; a message left in the grave read: 'Finally, O Duce, you are with us. We will cover you with roses, but the smell of your virtue will overpower those roses.'

Four months later what remained of *Il Duce* was found in a small trunk just outside Milan and two Franciscan monks were charged with hiding his body. In the intervening months the corpse had been kept on the move, variously hidden in a villa, a monastery and a convent. He was buried a second time in an undisclosed location, only to be dug up yet again eleven years later and returned to his widow Rachele, who buried him again in Predappio in 1957. Mussolini's brain, however, had been removed and shipped to the United States in 1945 for scientific experimentation to see if it shed any light on the human condition: it didn't.

The Bluegrass Hitler

The names of the Nigerian dictator Sani Abacha and his widow Maryam were frequently evoked in hoax emails naming them as the source of non-existent African money. The most courageous mail order con involving a dictator began in 1946, a year after Hitler's death, and lasted for over a decade.

William Johnson, a coal miner and part-time Baptist preacher from Kentucky, decided to cash in on rumours sweeping America that Hitler had been smuggled out of Berlin after the Russian army moved in and was alive and well and living in North America. Johnson, posing as Hitler, claimed that he had settled in Kentucky with some of his Nazi chiefs of staff, and was planning to take over the United States, made a public appeal for cash to help his cause.

It generated a steady stream of postal orders from Nazi sympathisers to help fund his dastardly plans for space ships, 'invisible ships' and underground hordes of ammunition.

Johnson had scammed over $10,000 dollars from the American public before an alert postal inspector spotted that Hitler's signature was a forgery. Johnson had been signing himself The Furrier instead of *The Führer*.

Laughter not the best medicine

By living to 82, Kim Jong-Il outlived the average citizen of North Korea by over 12 years, but he had hoped to make it to at least 120 and employed a team of 200 scientists to ensure that he became the world's longest living man.

Kim's research team concluded that he needed to laugh at least five times a day and laid on comedic entertainment for the leader including five and six year-olds "doing adorable things." These performances were followed by blood transfusions from younger men and food supplements involving 1,750 different herbs.

His death 2011 from a massive heart attack was linked to high blood pressure and diabetes fuelled by expensive dining habits: his $700,000 a year cognac bill can't have helped boost his life expectancy either.

Death of the undead

Even by Haitian standards, 'Papa Doc' Duvalier was highly superstitious. He made all of his most important decisions on the twenty-second day of the month, his 'lucky day' on which he believed he was guarded by his voodoo spirits. He once placed a voodoo curse on US President John F Kennedy and was delighted when JFK was assassinated on 22 November 1963, a coincidence that greatly enhanced the reputation of his alleged voodoo powers.

In his later years, Papa Doc only ever dared leave his presidential palace on the 22nd of the month. Although he liked to compare himself to the undead, Papa Doc stayed dead after succumbing to fatal diabetes in April 1971. The announcement of his passing was made on 22 April, by which time had already been dead for several days.

Heil honey, I'm home

In 1983 the German magazine *Stern* paid £2.3 million (about £50 a word) for 'the publishing scoop of the century', sixty-two volumes of Adolf Hitler's diaries dated from 1932 to 1945, covering the complete Third Reich.

The remarkable volumes, *Stern* reported, were recovered by some farmers from the wreckage of plane crash at the end of the war and had eventually made their way into the hands of *Stern* investigative reporter, Gerd 'the Detective' Heidemann.

Suspiciously, the diaries shed little light on the momentous events of the age and were mostly a collection of banal personal musings; a typical excerpt dated June 1935 read: 'Eva now has two dogs, so she won't get bored.'

An entry from December 1938: 'Now a year is nearly over. Have I achieved my goals for the Reich? Save for a few small details, yes!'

Another, during the 1936 Berlin Olympics: "Eva wants to come to the Games in Berlin, have had tickets delivered to her and her girlfriends. Hope my flatulence doesn't return during the Games."

Voices of skepticism were raised. Hitler, it was pointed out, famously hated taking notes, and was unlikely to have kept a diary. The diary covers were also decorated with the brass Gothic initials 'FH', the author having apparently mistaken the Gothic capital 'F' for an 'A' when he bought the type.

Nevertheless, the diaries were vouched as genuine by the great and much respected English historian Hugh Trevor-Roper, who declared, "I'm staking my reputation on it".

A few months later they were exposed as a clumsy modern forgery, written in the back room of a Stuttgart shop by Konrad Kujau, a small time dealer in Nazi memorabilia.

Herr Kujau's earlier creations included a sequel to *Mein Kampf*, several poems by Adolf Hitler and the beginnings of a Hitlerian opera entitled *Wieland der Schmied* - Wieland the Blacksmith.

Trial by television

The fall of Nicolae and Elena Ceausescu was the first revolution to be shown live on TV.

In December 1989 Ceausescu tried to address a mass rally in front of the Central Committee building in Bucharest. By the time of this, his final public speech, enthusiasm for 'the Most Loved and Esteemed Son and Daughter of the Romanian People' had dwindled so much that the applause had to be taped. For the first time in his career, Ceausescu was even rudely interrupted in mid-sentence by shouts of disapproval.

Clearly shocked, but egged on by his wife, he tried to finish his speech, but then, as the tape with pre-recorded applause and cheers was abruptly switched off, they decided to make a run for it.

The presidential couple were captured attempting to flee the capital by helicopter. They were quickly tried and convicted by a military tribunal on charges of mass murder and theft, and executed by a firing squad on Christmas Day, the soldiers firing so enthusiastically that they accidentally shot each other. After the freshly bleeding corpses of Nicolae and Elena were shown on TV as proof that their reign was over, they were wrapped in tent cloth, bundled aboard a waiting helicopter and dropped in the middle of a sports stadium in a Bucharest suburb. The following morning, to all round embarrassment, the corpses went missing. They turned up later in a nearby shed.

X-branded

In 1998 Adolf Hitler enjoyed an unlikely second career in Thailand, promoting pototo chips.

In a TV advertisement, Hitler eats some "X" brand chips and is transformed into a 'good' person. The ad ends with him stripping off his Nazi uniform and dancing around in his underwear. In a classy final touch, a swastika morphs into the brand 'X' logo. The advert was taken off the air following an outcry from critics including the Israeli Embassy in Bangkok.

Rest in pieces

In 1987 the hands and genitals of the Argentinean president Juan Peron were amputated and were subject to a £5 million ransom demand. Fortunately Peron had no further use for them, as he had already been dead for thirteen years.

Fruit loop

Idi Amin's reign of terror was ended on 11 April 1979 when an invading force of Ugandan exiles and Tanzanians forced 'Big Daddy' to flee to Egypt. When police searched the deposed leader's home they found a large case full of old film reels of *Tom and Jerry* cartoons stashed under his bed, next to boxes of hand grenades.

Twenty-five years later, the Italian journalist Riccardo Orizio interviewed Amin at his home in the Saudi city of Jidda, where the former dictator, now a devout Muslim and dedicated family man, liked to fish, play the organ and exercise at a local gym. He also discovered that Amin had acquired a new nickname, 'Dr. Jaffa'. It came from his excessive consumption of oranges: the former cannibal had turned fruitarian, believing that they would act like Viagra for him.

Orizio asked, did he feel any remorse for his eight-year rule that saw 300,000 people murdered, some of the victims reportedly fed to crocodiles, leaving Uganda's economy in total ruin? "Only nostalgia", Amin replied.

Amin died of multiple organ failure in 2003 with his favourite, ever-present portrait above his bed; that of a kilted King George VI or, as Amin knew him, 'my old commander-in-chief'.

The Honourable Mr. Hitler

In 2010, seventy-seven years after it was granted, the town of Dülmen in Germany finally got round to revoking Adolf Hitler's honorary citizenship.

Over 4,000 cities, towns and communities awarded honorary titles to Hitler during his time in power, many to mark his 44th birthday in 1933.

PROFILE: MAO ZEDONG

Born: 26 December 1893

Died: 9 September 1976

Also known as: Chairman Mao; The Great Helmsman

Occupation: Chairman of the People's Republic of China 1949 - 1976

Hobbies: swimming and recreational sex, both well into his eighties

Career highlight: telling whopping lies about his heroism in the Long March; (2) banned *The Sound Of Music*, "a blatant example of capitalist pornography"

Career lowlight: over-filled with embalming fluid when he died in 1976, his head burst

Significant others: four wives, most notably Jiang Qing - Madame Mao

Style: regulation grey military-style Mao suit, previously known as the Sun Yet-sen suit

Personality cult status: as totalitarian ruler of one quarter of the world's population, Mao - or 'No.1' as he would have been known had thing turned out differently - considered getting rid of people's names and replacing them with numbers. He thought it would make China's 550

☠ The Little Book of Loony Dictators ☭

million peasants more obedient workers

Whimsical cruelty factor:
truly creative in the field of human torture, gave his enemies enemas of Lysol toilet cleaning fluid (which destroyed their intestines) or ran piano wire through their penises.

☠ The Little Book of Loony Dictators ☠

PROFILE: KIM JONG-UN

Born: 8 January 1983. A child prodigy, he could drive at the age of three and was winning yachting races at nine, according to state official sources.[1]

Also known as: 'Brilliant Comrade' or 'Kim the third-generation pig' according to a popular title previously blocked on Chinese search engine Baidu.

Occupation: Supreme Leader of Democratic People's Republic of Korea 2011 -

Hobbies: looking at stuff and sometimes pointing. Also fond of baseball: in 2013 Kim met ex-NBA star Dennis Rodman – most likely the first American he had ever met. When Rodman visited Kim's private island he noted insightfully: "It's like Hawaii or Ibiza, but he's the only one that lives there."

Career highlight: at 26 he succeeded his late father and became the third member of the Kim family to rule the unpredictable and reclusive communist nation and the world's youngest head of state. He became the designated heir after his elder brother, Kim Jong-nam, fell out of favour after being arrested in Tokyo in 2001 while travelling to Disneyland on a forged passport.

Career lowlight: in September 2014 Kim disappeared temporarily from the public eye amid rumours of a cheese overdose. It was speculated that the North Korean dictator had become so fat that his ankles have fractured under his own weight.

Significant others: wife Ri Sol-ju, daughter Kim Ju-ae

Style: his trademark sweptback bouffant with shaved sides is known in North Korea as the "ambitious" style. In a country ravaged by famine, Kim remains a defiantly plump 20 stones. According to leaks sprung by Chinese diplomats linked to insiders within the

---

[1] Clearly a chip off the old block; his father Kim Jong-il reportedly learned to walk at just three weeks and was talking at eight weeks.

🐨 The Little Book of Loony Dictators 🔑

DPRK, Kim had plastic surgery years ago in order to look like more his grandfather Kim Il-Sung

Personality cult status: :

ordered people who share his name to change theirs. In 2012 a top military official was found drunk during the mourning period for Kim's father and was executed by mortar round after Kim gave the order to leave "no trace of him behind, down to his hair."

Whimsical cruelty factor:

had his 60 year old uncle publicly arrested and executed, the most high-profile casualty in a purge of top officials. Jang Song Thaek, according to Pyongyang's official newspaper, was guilty of "counter-revolutionary" acts and was "human scum" and "worse than a dog." Undercover reporters in North Korea described how some of Kim's purged enemies were also being killed by rocket grenade then incinerated by a flamethrower.

AUTHORITATIVE SOURCES

Almond, Mark - *The Rise and Fall of Nicolae and Elena Ceausescu* (Chapmans Publishers, 1992)

Axelrod, Alan and Phillips, Charles - *Dictators and Tyrants: Absolute Rulers and Would-Be Rulers in World History* (Facts on File Inc., 1995)

Bullock, Alan - *Hitler and Stalin: Parallel Lives* (Fontana Press, 1998)

Cawthorne, Nigel - *The Empress of South America* (Arrow, 2003)

Chang, Jung and Halliday, Jon - *Mao: The Unknown Story* (Jonathan Cape, 2005)

Decalo, Samuel - *Psychoses of Power: African Personal Dictatorships* (Westview Press, 1989)

Diederich, Bernard - *Papa Doc: Haiti and Its Dictator* (Penguin Books, 1972)

Diederich, Bernard - *Trujillo: The Death of the Dictator* (Markus Wiener Publishers, 2000)

Ferguson, James - *Papa Doc, Baby Doc* (Blackwell Publishers, 1988)

Gimlett, John - *At the Tomb of the Inflatable Pig: Travels Through Paraguay* (Arrow, 2004)

Kamau, Joseph and Cameron, Andrew - *Lust to Kill: Rise and Fall of Idi Amin* (Corgi Books, 1979)

Kershaw, Ian - *Hitler, 1889-1936: Hubris* (Penguin Books, 2001)

Kershaw, Ian - *Hitler, 1936-1945: Nemesis* (Penguin Books, 2001)

Li, Zhisui et al - *The Private Life of Chairman Mao* (Random House, 1996)

Norman, Philip - *Awful Moments* (Penguin Books, 1986)

Llosa, Mario Vargas - *The Feast of the Goat* (Faber and Faber, 2003)

Orizio, Riccardo - *Talk of the Devil: Encounters with Seven Dictators* (Vintage, 2004)

Pacepa, Ion Mihai - *Red Horizons: The True Story of Nicolae and Elena Ceausescu's Crimes, Lifestyle and Corruption* (Regnery Gateway, 1990)

Sebag-Montefiore, Simon - *Stalin: The Court of the Red Tsar* (Weidenfeld and Nicholson, 2003)

Smith, Denis Mack - *Mussolini* (Weidenfeld and Nicolson, 2001)

Smith, George Ivan - *Ghosts of Kampala: Rise and Fall of Idi Amin* (HarperCollins, 1980)

Wrong, Michela - *In the Footsteps of Mr. Kurtz: Living on the Brink of Disaster in Mobutu's Congo* (Perennial, 2002)

INDEX

Abacha, Sani, President of Nigeria 89, 157

AC/DC, song to oust dictator with 78

Ahmadinejad, Mahmoud, President of Iran 132

AIDs, magic cure for 63

Amin, Idi
and Princess Anne 1
and suffocation by handkerchief 4
and cannibalism 6, 19
and fondness for kilts 8
and sledgehammers 9
and Edward Heath 15
and cabinet meetings 17, 101
profile 20 - 21
and Queen Elizabeth II 51, 64, 101
and Princess Margaret 62
and international relations 7, 13, 60, 85
and wives 89 - 90
and TV documentary 101
and boxing career 112
and his legacy 162 - 163

assassination attempts
with a bazooka 41
with bombs 7, 149
with 'dirty' wet suit 41
with exploding conch 41
with guns 10, 28, 61
with pen-syringe 41
with poison 41

Babangida, President of Nigeria 24

Baby Doc (see Duvalier, Jean-Claude)

Balaguer, Joaquin, President of Dominican Republic 71

Banda, Hastings
and feeding opponents to crocodiles 7
and visit to Buckingham Palace 24
and Anglophilia 38
and Tom Jones 131

Batista, Fulgencio 51

beards, bans on 38, 40, 74

beards, false 28, 154

beards, plot to make fall out 41

Beria, Lavrenti 153 - 154

Betancourt, Romulo, President of Venezuela 149

Bible, use as toilet paper 50

Big Daddy (see Amin, Idi)

Bokassa, Jean-Bédel
    and table manners 8, 55,
    and school uniforms 11
    and beggars 13
    profile 22 - 23
    and coronation banquet 55 - 56
    and overthrow 128

bras, bulletproof 89

Braun Eva
    and wedding day 85
    and Hollywood 85
    and fur coats 85
    and sex life with Adolf 135

cats, dictators with fear of 131

Carol II, King of Romania 115

Castro, Fidel 41 - 42, 69

Ceaucescu, Elena
    and visit to Buckingham Palace 24, 48
    and fear of germs 31
    and children 39, 92
    and career as a scientist 86 - 87
    and blackmailing officials 92
    and Romanian TV 160
    and execution 160 - 161

Ceausescu, Nicolae
    and free speech 23
    and personal food taster 24
    and visit to Buckingham Palace 24 - 25
    and bugging devices 22, 25, 62
    and paranoia 22, 30, 36
    and his dog 37
    and birth control 39
    and his father 40
    profile 43 - 44
    and the Ceausescu Diet 54
    and building projects 65
    and bear hunting 113
    and execution 160 - 161

Chung Hee, Park 11, 38

CIA, attempts to kill Fidel Castro 41 - 42

Clinton, Bill 37

Colonel Trunk (see Stroessner, Alfredo)

crocodiles, feeding enemies to 7, 162

dictators, embalmed 151, 156,

Diem, Ngo Dinh 8

dolphins, bathing in the blood of 117

Duvalier, Jean-Claude 56 - 57, 78

Duvalier, Francoise
dwarf, specialist in biting off genitals 2
and voodoo 3, 68
and attempts to over throw 34 - 35
and Tonton Macoutes 16
profile 45 - 46
and stealing foreign aid 50 - 51
and medals 51
and travel industry 52
and vote rigging 53
and Duvalierville 55
and Haile Selassie 68
and Christianity 71
and writing career 99
and cars 141
and superstition 158 - 159

Edinburgh, Duke of
and Idi Amin 51
and *Mein Kampf* 98
and General Stroessner 145

El Jefe (see Trujillo, Rafael)

El Lider (see Peron, Juan)

El Mariscal (see Lopez, Francisco Solano)

El Supremo (see Francia, Jose Gaspar Rodriguez)

Equatorial Guinea 2, 12, 73, 100, 155,

Fahd, King of Saudi Arabia 24

Francia, Jose Gaspar Rodriguez 26, 150

Franco, General 5, 152 - 153

freezer, body parts kept in 22, 41

flatulence, dictators suffering from 126 - 127, 130, 135, 159

floorboards, predecessors kept under 3

Gaddafi, Muammar
profile 47 - 48
and writing career 100
and football 116
and flatulence 130
and his teddy bear 138
and penis-lengthening 138

golf club, beaten to death with 118

Great Helmsman (see Zedong, Mao)

heads
staved in 7
bursting 163

Heath, Edward 15, 79

heavy metal, correct usage of 78

Hitler, Adolf
  and medication 5 - 6
  and bombing England 6
  and his death ray 9
  and fans of 12, 20, 72, 73
  and his father 19
  and potty training 34
  and his doubles 35 - 36
  profile 58 - 59
  and horses 64
  and wedding day 85
  and *Mein Kampf* 97 - 98
  and painting 99 - 100
  and physical fitness 112 - 113
  and flatulence 126
  and his sister-in-law 128 - 129
  and Blondi 131
  and taste in music 131
  and sex life 133 - 135
  and eyesight 135
  and Mickey Mouse 136
  and smoking 139 - 14
  and cars 140
  and Henry Ford 140
  and missing testicle 152
  and General Franco 152
  and penis 154
  and his diaries 159 - 160
  and TV sponsorship 161
  and legacy 162

Hitler, Bridget 128 - 129

Hoxha, Enver
  and relations with prime minister 9
  and paranoia 32
  and concrete bunkers 32
  and his double 35
  and beards 38
  and various bans 39, 131,
  profile 60 - 61
  and speeches 98
  and Norman Wisdom 127
  and his diet 129
  and his death 154

Hussein, Uday 18 - 19, 102, 128

Hussein, Saddam
  and etiquette at cabinet meetings 2
  and his sons 18
  fear of germs 31
  profile 81 - 82
  and torture methods 82
  and writing novels 102 - 103
  and footwear 133
  and *The Godfather* 138

Ilyumzhinov, President of Kalmykia 76

Il Sung, Kim
  and durability 4
  and faeces 33
  and US intelligence 40
  and personality cult 69
  and highway code 142
  and war record 69
  and his mausoleum 151

Jammeh, president of Gambia 62 - 63

Jong Il, Kim
   and bowel and bladder movements, lack of 34
   and fear of triplets 37
   and doubles 37
   and conspicuous consumption 49
   and gardening skills 73
   profile 83 - 84
   and post-coital karaoke 78
   and North Korean film industry 101 - 102
   and prolific writing 103
   and golf prowess 110
   and his favourite food 131
   and western films 138 - 139
   and death of 128, 158

Khrushchev, Nikita 27, 69, 93, 155,

legs, false 75 - 76

Lenin, Vladimir Ilyich 141, 150 - 151

long hair, bans on 38

Lopez, Francisco Solano 28- 29, 62, 91- 92

Lukashenko, Alexander
   and Hitler 72
   profile 94
   and sporting prowess 115

Lynch, Eliza 91 - 92

Madame Mao (see Qing Jiang)

Marcos, Ferdinand
   and kickbacks 54
   profile 95 - 96

Marcos, Imelda
   and mystical visions 86
   and karaoke 88
   and The Beatles 88
   and shoes 89
   and allergy to ugliness 93

Martínez, President of El Salvador 63 - 64

Miriam, Mengistu 3

Mobutu, Joseph
   and shopping trips 49
   and supernatural feats 66 - 67
   and women 92
profile 104 - 105

Mugabe, Robert
   profile 106 - 107

Mussolini, Benito
   and superstition 26
   and taking himself a bit too seriously 67
   and swearing 68
   and career as a novelist 98
   profile 108 - 109
   and sporting prowess 112
   and spaghetti 127 - 128

and health problems 130
and fashion 136
and syphilis 137
and his death 156 - 157

Nazis, gay 134 - 135

Ne Win, General
and superstition 27
and birth control 39
profile 117 - 118

Nguema, Macias
and soundtrack to executions 2
and use of hallucinogens 73
and inferiority complex 100 - 101

Niyazov, Saparmurat
and international relations 68
and abolishing the calendar 74
profile 119 - 120
and smoking 140

Noriega, Manuel, President of Panama 77 - 78

Nyere, Julius, President of Tanzania 5, 112

Operation Condor 4

Pastor, Coronel 5

Papa Doc (see Duvalier, Francoise)

penis, Hitler's 154

Peron, Eva 90 - 91

Peron, Juan
profile 121 - 122
and body parts 161

Persia, Shah of 24

pets 37, 42, 58, 104

piano wire, torture with 157

pigs, barbecued in Buckingham Palace 24

Pot, Pol
profile 123 - 124

Qing Jiang, 'Madam Mao' 85 - 86, 88

Richard, Sir Cliff 132

Somoza, Anastasio, President of Nicaragua 111, 149

Santa Anna, Antonio Lopez de 75 - 76

sharks, feeding enemies to 148

Shehu, Mehmet 9

Stalin, Josef
and bananas 13
and witticisms 18, 70
and health problems 25
and drinking contests 27
and his doubles 36
and his rallies 78
and favorite films 125

and jazz music 131
and boot fetish 132 - 133
and cars 141
profile 143 - 144
and his death 153 - 154
and his legacy 155

Selassie, Haile 3, 68

Stroessner, Alfredo
and Operation Condor 4
and his secret police 5
profile 145 - 146

Suicide Sarah 90

testicles, missing 137, 152 - 153, 156, 164

testicles, touching of 108

Tonton Macoutes 16 - 17, 46, 51

torture methods 2, 4, 5, 24, 28, 48, 107, 109, 114, 120, 146

Trujillo, Rafael
and torture techniques 2
and medal awards 3
and secret police 12
and kidnapping 15 - 16
and daughter's wedding 53
and nickname of 64
and baseball 110 - 111
profile 147 - 148
and death of 149 - 150

Uncle Joe (see Stalin, Josef)

Wisdom, Norman 127

yogurts named after dictators 120

Zedong, Mao
and poetry writing 10
and sparrows 14
and comfy chairs 17
and jokes 26
and paranoia 32 - 33
and toilet habits 33
and Idi Amin 62
and personality cult 66
and mangoes 77
and senility 79 - 80
and Little Red Book 98 - 99
and table tennis 112
and swimming 116
and hygiene 129 - 130
and *The Sound Of Music* 131
and the Mao suit 135 - 136
and sex life 136 - 137
and smoking 139
and cars 141
profile 163 - 164

Zog, King of Albania 29 - 31, 49